Problem Solving for Kids

A Smart Guide to Thinking and Fixing Things

Table of Contents

Introduction

Problems are part of life. You face them at home, at school, and with friends. Some are small, like a missing pencil. Others feel big, like a bad grade or a fight. Every problem asks one question: *What will you do next?*

This book helps you answer that question. It shows you how to think clearly, stay calm, and act with purpose. Problem-solving is not magic. It's a skill you build step by step. You learn it by asking the right questions and trying different ways to fix what's wrong.

You will learn how to find the real issue, not just what's easy to see. You'll learn to break big problems into smaller ones so they don't feel so heavy. You'll also learn how to test your ideas, look at facts, and plan ahead.

Solving problems starts with a mindset. You don't wait for someone else to fix things. You take action. You ask, "What's really going on here?" and "What can I do right now?" That attitude turns confusion into progress.

Each chapter in this book gives you one clear lesson. Some chapters teach you how to think. Others help you plan or work with people. Together they build a way of thinking that helps you in school, in sports, and in daily life.

You don't need to be perfect. You only need to be curious and keep trying. Every problem is a chance to learn something new about how the world works and how you think. By the end of this book, you'll have a set of tools to use whenever things go wrong or feel hard.

Take your time. Read one chapter at a time. Try the exercises. Notice how small changes in your thinking make big changes in your results.

You're not learning how to avoid problems. You're learning how to face them with skill and confidence.

SECTION 1:
Foundations of Problem-Solving

Every skill needs a base. Problem-solving starts with how you think before you act. This section teaches you to slow down, ask smart questions, and see what's really going on. You'll learn to look past what's obvious, spot what matters most, and set goals that make sense.

The goal is simple: think with purpose before you move. Once you learn these habits, every other part of solving problems becomes easier.

Chapter 1: Ask the Right Question

Every problem starts with a question. The kind of question you ask shapes the path you take. If your question is unclear, your answer will be too. But if your question is focused, you'll know where to begin.

Think about when you lose something. You might ask, "Where's my book?" That's a start, but it's broad. A stronger question is, "Where did I last see my book?" or "Who borrowed it today?" That kind of question points you toward action.

Questions guide your thinking. They open doors you didn't see before. When you face a problem, stop and ask yourself what you *need* to know. Good questions turn a confusing situation into a clear one. Bad questions waste time.

Here are a few types of questions that help you think better:

- **Fact questions**: What do I already know for sure?
- **Cause questions**: Why did this happen?
- **Action questions**: What can I do next?
- **Goal questions**: What do I want to happen instead?

Each kind of question shows a new piece of the puzzle. Together they help you see the full picture.

When you ask questions, keep them short. Long, complicated questions slow your thinking. Say one idea at a time. For example, "What caused this mistake?" is stronger than "What caused this mistake, who made it, and why didn't anyone notice sooner?"

Also, avoid questions that blame. "Who messed this up?" shuts people down. "How can we fix this?" gets people talking. Problem-solving works best when everyone feels safe to think and share.

If you're stuck, write down everything you don't understand. Then turn each point into a question. You'll see how the problem starts to make sense.

Here's a quick exercise: Think about a small problem in your day, maybe a homework issue or a plan that went wrong. Write five questions about it. Then read them again and circle the one that seems most helpful. That's your starting point.

You'll notice that strong questions are often calm and curious, not emotional. They help you think before you react. When you train yourself to ask better questions, you give yourself more control.

The best thinkers in science, business, and art all start here. They don't guess first; they ask first. Every clear question is a step toward a clear answer.

So, next time you face a problem, don't rush to fix it. Sit quietly for a moment and ask: "What's the right question here?" Once you find that question, the solution will follow.

Chapter 2: Define the Real Problem

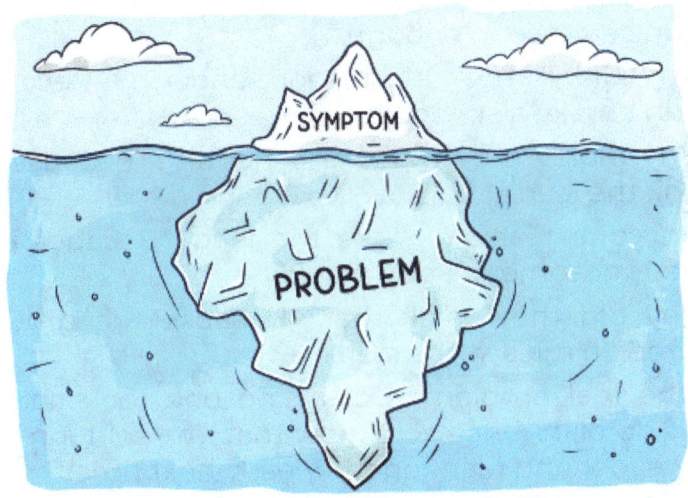

You can't solve what you don't understand. Before you start fixing things, you need to know exactly what the problem is. Many people skip this step. They rush to fix what's in front of them, and then wonder why the same problem comes back.

Defining the real problem means slowing down and looking closer. It's like a detective studying clues before making a move. You might think you know the issue, but often what you see first is only a small part of it.

Think about this example: your group project at school didn't get finished on time. You might say the problem is "we ran out of time." But that's not the real issue. Maybe the group didn't plan early enough. Maybe people didn't share the work evenly. Maybe no one checked progress until the last minute. The missed deadline is a *result*, not the real problem.

To define the real problem, ask a few simple questions:

- What exactly went wrong?
- When did it start?
- Who or what is affected?
- Why is it happening again?

Then keep asking "why" until you reach the cause that makes sense. It's called "the five whys" method. You ask "why" about five times to peel away the layers.

Here's how it works:

1. The class project was late. Why? Because the group didn't start soon enough.
2. Why didn't they start soon enough? Because they didn't make a schedule.
3. Why didn't they make a schedule? Because no one took the lead.
4. Why didn't anyone take the lead? Because everyone thought someone else would.
5. Why did they think that? Because the group didn't agree on roles at the start.

Now the real problem is clear: no one took charge, and there was no plan. Once you know that, the solution is simple: choose a leader and plan together early next time.

This step might sound slow, but it saves time later. If you fix only the surface issue, the problem will return. When you fix the cause, it stays fixed.

You can practice this every day. When something goes wrong, write down what happened. Then list what caused it. Keep digging until you find the point where one small change could stop it from happening again.

Here's a quick exercise: Think of something that didn't work out this week. Write one sentence about what happened. Then write five "why" questions about it. When you reach the last one, look at your answer. That's usually the real problem.

Good problem solvers don't guess. They define. Once you see what's really wrong, the right answer becomes clear. Defining the real problem gives you direction, and direction turns confusion into action.

Chapter 3: Separate Symptoms from Causes

Sometimes a problem looks big because you're seeing the symptoms, not the cause. A symptom is what you notice. A cause is what makes it happen. If you fix only the symptom, the problem keeps coming back. If you fix the cause, the problem goes away for good.

Think of it like getting a cold. The runny nose and sore throat are symptoms. The virus is the cause. You can wipe your nose all day, but until your body fights the virus, you won't feel better. Problems work the same way.

At school, imagine you're late for class three times in one week. The symptom is being late. The cause could be your alarm, your bedtime, or how you get ready in the morning. If you only try to walk faster to class, you're fixing the symptom. If you start setting your alarm earlier, you're fixing the cause.

To separate symptoms from causes, try this three-step process:

1. **List what you can see.**

   These are the signs, the things that show something is wrong. For example: missed deadlines, poor grades, or arguments with teammates.

2. **Ask what makes those signs happen.**

   For each symptom, ask "Why is this happening?" Keep digging until you reach a reason that doesn't depend on another problem.

3. **Focus your effort on the cause, not the surface.**

   You can still handle the symptoms, but spend most of your energy fixing the root.

Here's another example. Your friend says group work is boring. That's a symptom. You ask why. They say no one listens to their ideas. That's a cause. You ask again why. They say people keep interrupting. The deeper cause might be poor communication. Now you know what to work on: how to listen better as a team.

Try this quick exercise: Pick a small problem you've noticed this week. Write down what's bothering you. That's the symptom. Then write down what you think is making it happen. That's the cause. Keep asking "why" until you reach the first thing that sets everything else in motion.

You'll notice that most real problems sit underneath the surface. They're not as easy to see, but they're worth finding. When you learn to tell the difference between what you see and what's behind it, you stop wasting time on quick fixes. You start solving what matters.

Strong problem-solvers don't guess at causes. They look, ask, and test until the real one appears. Once you find the cause, every step after that becomes easier.

Chapter 4: Break It Down: Divide and Conquer

Big problems can feel heavy. When you look at everything at once, it's easy to freeze or give up. The trick is to break the problem into smaller parts. When you solve one piece at a time, the problem starts to shrink.

Imagine your teacher gives you a science project due in three weeks. At first, it feels like too much. But when you break it down, it's not so bad. You might split it into steps:

1. Pick a topic.
2. Do the research.
3. Write your notes.
4. Create the experiment.
5. Build your display.
6. Practice your presentation.

Now it's clear. Each step is something you can handle in a day or two.

Breaking problems into smaller parts helps you see progress. Every small win builds confidence. You go from "I can't do this" to "I've finished the first step." That small change in thinking makes a big difference.

Here's how to start:

1. **Write the problem at the top of your page.**

   Make it one clear sentence.

2. **List the smaller parts underneath.**

   Ask, "What needs to happen first?" and "What depends on what?"

3. **Tackle one part at a time.**

   When you finish one, cross it off and move to the next.

Try this example. Say your goal is to clean your messy room. Instead of seeing it as one giant task, divide it into zones: desk, closet, floor, and shelves. Set a timer for fifteen minutes per zone. You'll move faster and see results right away.

This skill works everywhere. In sports, you learn one move before the next. In music, you practice one line at a time. In math, you solve part of a problem before the whole equation.

Here's a short exercise: Think of something that feels too big to handle, maybe studying for a big test or fixing a friendship that's been rough. Write down the problem. Then list three smaller parts of it you can start with today. Choose one and do it.

Breaking things down doesn't mean the problem is smaller. It means you're smarter about how you face it. One small piece at a time leads to full solutions. That's how every big thing gets done: step by step, piece by piece.

The best problem-solvers don't try to do everything at once. They divide, focus, and move forward. That's how you turn a mountain into a path you can walk.

Chapter 5: Stay Curious, Not Judgmental

When something goes wrong, it's easy to point fingers. You might think, "Someone messed up," or "This is unfair." But blaming stops you from learning. Curiosity helps you move forward.

Being curious means asking questions before making conclusions. It means saying, "I wonder why this happened," instead of, "Whose fault is this?" When you stay curious, you open the door to new answers. When you judge too soon, you close it.

Let's look at an example. You're doing a group project, and your friend forgets to send their part on time. If you judge, you might say, "They're lazy." If you stay curious, you might ask, "Did they understand what to do?" or "Did something stop them from finishing?" One response blames. The other seeks to understand.

Curiosity helps you see the full story. You learn what's behind people's choices and what might fix the problem for everyone. Judgment makes people feel small. Curiosity invites them in.

Here's a short way to stay curious:

1. **Pause before reacting.**

   Take one breath. Then ask a question.

2. **Assume there's more to learn.**

   Most problems have hidden parts you can't see yet.

3. **Ask calm questions.**

   "What happened?" "What made that hard?" "What could we try next time?"

4. **Listen to the answers.**

   Don't rush to talk. Listen until the other person finishes.

You can practice this anywhere. When you disagree with someone, ask what they were thinking. When something breaks, ask how it works instead of who broke it. Every question teaches you something new.

Try this quick exercise. Think of a time when you felt frustrated with someone. Write what happened. Then write three questions that could help you understand them better. Read your questions out loud. Notice how your thinking changes when you shift from blame to curiosity.

Curiosity doesn't mean letting people off the hook. It means finding the truth before reacting. It helps you fix problems without hurting feelings.

When you stay curious, people trust you more. They see that you want to solve things, not attack them. That trust makes problem-solving faster and kinder.

Strong problem-solvers keep their minds open. They don't jump to blame. They ask, learn, and then act. Curiosity keeps your brain working and your heart calm. It helps you see not only what went wrong, but how to make it right.

Chapter 6: Clarify the Desired Outcome

Before you start solving a problem, you need to know what success looks like. If you don't, you might work hard and still miss the goal. Clear outcomes guide your effort. They tell you what to aim for and when to stop.

An outcome is the result you want. It's the finish line. Without it, you wander in circles. With it, you move straight ahead.

Let's say your soccer team keeps losing games. You might say, "We need to get better." That's too vague. What does "better" mean? Scoring more goals? Passing faster? Working as a team? A clear outcome sounds like this: "We want to improve our passing so we keep the ball longer." Now you have something you can measure and practice.

Here's how to clarify your desired outcome:

1. **Say what you want to happen.**

    Write one sentence that starts with "I want…" or "We want…" Make it specific.

2. **Add details that show what success means.**

   Use numbers, times, or clear signs of progress.

3. **Check if it's possible.**

   Your outcome should challenge you, but still be within reach.

4. **Keep it short and simple.**

   If you can't explain your goal in one breath, it's too long.

Here's an example. Instead of saying, "I want to do better in school," say, "I want to raise my math grade from a C to a B by the next report card." The second one gives you direction. You can now plan how much to study, what to review, and when to ask for help.

Having a clear outcome also helps you stay focused. When new ideas or distractions come up, you can ask, "Will this help me reach my goal?" If not, skip it. That one question keeps your energy where it matters.

Try this quick exercise. Think of one problem you want to fix this month. Write down what a successful ending looks like. Then list three small actions that could lead there.

Clarity is power. When you know your target, your effort has purpose. You waste less time and make better choices.

Strong problem-solvers always know where they're headed before they begin. They picture the finish line, plan their steps, and then move with confidence. A clear outcome is your map. Without it, you wander. With it, you win.

Chapter 7: Know Your Constraints

Every problem has limits. You might not have enough time, money, tools, or help. These limits are called constraints. They don't stop you from solving the problem, but they shape how you solve it. Smart problem-solvers pay attention to what's possible before they start.

Think of constraints as the edges of a puzzle. They don't show you the full picture, but they help you know where to place the pieces. When you understand your limits, you can work inside them instead of fighting them.

Let's take an example. You have a science fair project due in one week. You want to build a robot that talks, but you don't have the parts or time. Instead of giving up, you can adjust. Maybe you build a model robot that moves its arms. You stay creative while working within your limits.

Knowing your constraints helps you plan smarter. It keeps you from wasting effort on ideas that won't work right now. It also pushes you to think creatively. When you can't do everything, you focus on what matters most.

Here's how to find your constraints:

1. **List your limits.**

    Write down what you don't have or can't do yet. Maybe it's time, tools, people, or money.

2. **Be honest.**

    Don't ignore limits or pretend they'll fix themselves.

3. **Work within what's real.**

    Plan with what's available today, not what you hope you'll get later.

4. **See limits as challenges, not walls.**

    Ask yourself, "What can I do with what I have?"

You can practice this every day. Say you're planning a class party, but you have only a small budget. You could complain about what's missing, or you could find low-cost games and decorations. Knowing your limits helps you find creative ways to still reach your goal.

Here's a short exercise: Think of a goal you're working on right now. List three limits that make it harder. Then write one idea for how you could work around each one. Maybe you can ask for help, trade tasks, or change the plan slightly.

Constraints don't stop creativity. They shape it. Some of the best inventions in history were made under tight limits. When people have fewer choices, they think more clearly.

Knowing your constraints doesn't mean giving up on big ideas. It means being smart about how to reach them. Once you understand your limits, you can use your time, energy, and tools wisely.

Strong problem-solvers don't waste time wishing for perfect conditions. They start with what they have, do what they can, and build from there. When you know your constraints, you control the challenge instead of letting it control you.

Chapter 8: Prioritize: What Matters Most?

When you face a big problem, it's easy to feel pulled in every direction. You might have ten things to fix and only enough time for three. That's when you need to prioritize. Prioritizing means choosing what matters most and working on it first.

You can't do everything at once. Trying to fix everything often means fixing nothing well. The best problem-solvers decide what deserves attention right now, and what can wait.

Start by asking yourself three questions:

1. What's most important to the goal?
2. What will make the biggest difference if I fix it first?
3. What can I do right now with the time and tools I have?

Let's look at an example. Imagine your class is planning a fundraiser. You need posters, volunteers, and snacks to sell. Everything feels urgent. But if no one books the event space, nothing else matters. So that task comes first. Once the space is ready, you can focus on signs, snacks, and setup.

Prioritizing doesn't mean ignoring smaller things. It means doing them later, in order. When you know your order, your energy goes where it counts. You work smarter, not harder.

Here's a way to practice: make a simple list of all your tasks. Then mark each one with a number:

- **1:** Must do today.
- **2:** Should do soon.
- **3:** Nice to do later.

Focus on the 1s first. When they're done, move to the 2s. Leave the 3s for free time or quiet days.

Here's another example. Let's say you have homework in three subjects. You could start with the one you like most, but that might not be wise. If your math test is tomorrow and your art project is due next week, start with math. Urgent tasks often matter most.

Prioritizing also helps in group work. Teams work better when everyone agrees on what comes first. If one person is focused on design and another on printing, the team might waste time. But if everyone agrees to finish the plan before starting design, the group moves smoothly.

Try this quick exercise. Think about something you're working on this week. Write all the steps on paper. Now number them by importance. Start with number one today.

Priorities change sometimes. Be ready to adjust if new information comes in. If a small issue suddenly blocks progress, it might move to the top of the list. Stay flexible but focused.

Knowing what matters most helps you use time wisely. It keeps you from jumping between tasks or losing energy on less important things. Every problem feels smaller when you know what to do first.

Strong problem-solvers don't rush into action. They stop, think, and choose. They know where their time will make the biggest impact. When you set clear priorities, you take control of your progress instead of letting your tasks control you.

Chapter 9: Spot Hidden Assumptions

Every time you face a problem, your brain fills in gaps with guesses. Those guesses feel true, but they aren't always right. They're called assumptions. Hidden assumptions can make a problem harder to solve because they shape how you see it before you even start thinking.

An assumption is something you believe without checking. Sometimes it's small, like thinking a friend is mad because they didn't text back. Sometimes it's big, like assuming a project will take one day when it really needs three. The trouble is that assumptions can lead you in the wrong direction.

Here's an example. Your group is building a model bridge for science class. You assume cardboard is strong enough. You start building, and halfway through, the bridge collapses. You lost time because you didn't test your guess first. The assumption wasn't evil; it was untested.

Good problem-solvers don't fight assumptions. They find them and test them. Once you know which ideas are facts and which are guesses, you can think clearly.

Here's how to spot hidden assumptions:

1. **Write what you believe about the problem.**

   Be honest. Don't skip things that seem obvious. Sometimes those are the most important.

2. **Ask yourself, "Do I know this is true?"**

   If you don't, mark it as a guess.

3. **Look for weak spots.**

   Which guesses could cause trouble if they're wrong?

4. **Test your guesses.**

   Ask questions, do research, or run small experiments before moving ahead.

Let's take another example. You assume your class can finish a group presentation in two days. Ask, "What makes me think that?" Maybe you're basing it on last time, when there were fewer slides. By checking that assumption early, you avoid last-minute stress.

Here's a short exercise. Think of a problem you're working on. Write three things you believe about it. Then ask yourself which ones are facts and which ones are guesses. For each guess, write one way to check it.

Spotting assumptions takes practice. The more you do it, the faster you catch them. You'll start noticing when your brain fills in blanks too quickly. That awareness keeps you from jumping to wrong conclusions.

Testing your assumptions doesn't make you slow. It makes you smart. It stops you from wasting effort on ideas that won't work.

Strong problem-solvers don't trust every thought that comes to mind. They check what's real. They ask for proof. They're curious about what they might be missing. That's what helps them see problems the way they truly are, not the way they first appear.

When you learn to spot hidden assumptions, you think more clearly and act with confidence. You stop guessing and start knowing.

Chapter 10: Embrace Uncertainty

No one likes not knowing what will happen. Uncertainty feels uncomfortable. It makes you want to rush for quick answers or avoid the problem altogether. But every real problem starts with some uncertainty. The best problem-solvers learn to stay calm when things aren't clear.

Uncertainty means you don't have all the facts yet. That's normal. It doesn't mean you're wrong or unprepared. It means you're in the middle of learning. Every scientist, inventor, and explorer begins there. They make guesses, test them, and learn from what happens next.

Think about when you start a new puzzle. At first, you have no idea where each piece fits. But if you keep looking, shapes and colors begin to make sense. The same happens with problems. The answers appear as you keep asking questions and trying small steps.

Here's how to handle uncertainty in a smart way:

1. **Accept it.**

   Tell yourself, "I don't know yet, but I'm learning."

2. **Start small.**

   Take one step that gives you more information. Then look at what you learned before taking the next step.

3. **Ask for input.**

   Talk to others. They may see what you can't.

4. **Stay flexible.**

   Be ready to adjust your plan when you learn something new.

Let's look at an example. You're joining a new club at school, and you don't know anyone. That's uncertain. You can't control who will talk to you, but you can take action. You might start by saying hello to one person. If they're friendly, you've learned something. If they're quiet, you try someone else. Each small action gives you new information, and soon the unknown becomes familiar.

Uncertainty also helps you grow. When you're not sure what will happen, your brain works harder. You pay more attention. You think more deeply. That's how you learn new skills.

Here's a short exercise. Think of something that feels uncertain right now. Write it down. Then write three things you can do to learn more about it. Maybe that's asking a teacher a question, doing a quick search, or testing one small idea.

The truth is that no one ever knows everything. Even experts face surprises. What matters is how you respond. You can freeze and worry, or you can stay calm and keep moving.

Strong problem-solvers don't wait for perfect information. They act, learn, and adjust. They understand that not knowing is part of solving. Every answer starts with a question, and every question begins with a little uncertainty.

When you stop fearing the unknown, you become braver. You start exploring instead of avoiding. Uncertainty stops being scary and starts feeling like a challenge. That's when real problem-solving begins.

SECTION 2:
Creative Problem-Solving

Once you understand the basics of how to think, it's time to get creative. Creative problem-solving means looking for new paths instead of walking the same old ones. It's about asking bold questions, mixing ideas, and trying things that might fail but also might work better than you expected.

You don't need to be an artist to think creatively. You only need to be curious and open-minded. This section helps you find fresh ways to look at problems, explore "what if" ideas, and turn imagination into action. Creativity isn't random. It's a skill you can practice every day.

Chapter 11: Brainstorm Like a Pro

Every great idea starts as a small thought. Brainstorming helps you bring those thoughts out of your head and onto paper. It's how you find new ways to solve problems before choosing the best one. The trick is to think wide first, then narrow later.

When you brainstorm, your goal is not to be right. Your goal is to be open. You want to come up with as many ideas as possible, even if they sound silly or strange. Some of the best inventions began as ideas that seemed odd at first.

Think of brainstorming as a game of "what else?" You start with one idea, then ask, "What else could work?" The more ideas you list, the more chances you have to find something great.

Here's how to brainstorm like a pro:

1. **Start with a clear question.**

    Know exactly what you're trying to solve. "How can we raise money for the school trip?" is better than "How can we help the school?"

2. **Set a short timer.**

    Try five or ten minutes. It keeps your energy up.

3. **Write everything down.**

   Don't trust your memory. Even wild ideas can help later.

4. **Say yes to every idea.**

   During brainstorming, there are no bad ideas. You can sort them later.

5. **Work with others.** In groups, build on each other's thoughts. Say "Yes, and..." instead of "No, but..."

6. **Take breaks.**

   Sometimes the best idea arrives after you stop thinking so hard.

Here's an example. Your class wants to plan a school fundraiser. You start listing ideas: bake sale, car wash, sports day, art auction, raffle, trivia night. Some sound normal, some sound funny. A classmate adds "costume fun run." Everyone laughs, but then someone says, "That's actually fun." You mix the ideas: a fun run with prizes for best costume. The idea works because no one shut it down too early.

Brainstorming works best when you feel free. That means no judging, no pressure, and no fear of being wrong. You can always cut ideas later, but you can't build on ideas that never get shared.

Here's a quick exercise. Think of something small that bugs you, maybe messy desks or long lines in the cafeteria. Set a timer for five minutes and write as many ideas as you can to fix it. Don't stop or erase anything. When time's up, read your list and circle the top three.

Good brainstorming feels messy. That's a sign it's working. A blank page means no progress. A crowded page means your brain is awake and active.

Strong problem-solvers use brainstorming to explore before deciding. They know that one idea often leads to another, and sometimes the best idea hides behind a silly one.

When you learn to brainstorm like a pro, you stop waiting for ideas to appear. You create them yourself. You fill the page, explore the wild ones, and let your imagination do the work. That's how creativity grows, one idea at a time.

Chapter 12: Think Outside the Box

Sometimes the best solution is not the one everyone expects. Thinking outside the box means looking beyond what is usual or easy. It means being brave enough to ask, "What if we tried something different?" when everyone else says, "This is how it's always done."

Creative thinkers are not afraid to explore. They know that new ideas often come from trying what others ignore. When you think differently, you find paths that others miss.

Here's an example. Your art club wants to raise money for new supplies. Most students say to sell paintings. That makes sense, but you wonder, "What if we teach a mini art class instead?" You could invite younger students, charge a small fee, and share what you love. That's thinking outside the box. It changes the question from "What can we sell?" to "How else can we share our talent?"

Here's how to build this skill:

1. **Ask "Why?" often.**

   Don't follow rules blindly. Ask why something is done a certain way. If no one has a good reason, try a new one.

2. **Look at the problem from another point of view.**

   Imagine how someone younger or older would see it.

3. **Change one thing.**

   What happens if you switch the order, location, or timing of something? A small change can lead to a big idea.

4. **Think about opposites.**

   If everyone is going one direction, ask what would happen if you tried the opposite.

You can practice this every day. Let's say you always study in your room. Try studying outside for one day. You might notice you focus better. If you always solve a math problem the same way, try drawing it instead. When you change your approach, your brain wakes up.

Here's a short exercise. Pick a problem that feels stuck. Write down the usual way people solve it. Then write three new ways, no matter how strange they sound. After that, choose one idea to test. You might find a solution no one has thought of yet.

Thinking outside the box doesn't mean being wild or random. It means being curious and open. It means giving yourself permission to ask questions that others skip.

Strong problem-solvers know that every great idea starts as something different. They don't stop at the first answer. They keep looking until they find one that truly works.

When you think outside the box, you give yourself more choices. You see new angles and fresh possibilities. The more you practice, the easier it becomes. Soon, thinking differently won't feel strange. It will feel natural.

Chapter 13: Use Analogies to Spark Ideas

An analogy helps you understand something new by comparing it to something you already know. It connects one idea to another and helps your brain find patterns. When you use analogies, you turn hard problems into ones that feel familiar.

An analogy is like a bridge between two thoughts. For example, you might say, "Solving a problem is like playing a puzzle." Each piece connects to another until you see the full picture. That picture makes sense because you already understand puzzles.

Using analogies helps you think creatively. They let you borrow ideas from one area and use them in another. A chef might learn something from a scientist about how to mix ingredients. A student might learn something about teamwork from watching a sports team. Ideas grow when they connect.

Here's how to use analogies to spark ideas:

1. **Think of something you already understand.** It could be a sport, a hobby, or a daily routine.

2. **Compare it to the problem you're solving.**

   Ask how they are similar.

3. **Look for lessons in that comparison.**

   What works in one situation that could work in the other?

4. **Test the idea.**

   Try it and see if the new way helps.

Here's an example. Suppose you are planning a school play, but rehearsals are chaotic. You think of your favorite soccer team. You realize that before every game, the team practices drills, sets positions, and reviews plays. You could use the same idea. Before each rehearsal, the group could warm up voices, assign parts, and run small sections first. The structure from sports helps theater run better.

Analogies help your brain see links that are easy to miss. They connect things that seem different but share the same rules. Engineers use them all the time. For example, early airplane wings were modeled after birds. By studying how birds move, inventors learned how to make machines fly.

Here's a short exercise. Think of a problem you're facing at school. Now think of something you enjoy, like music, sports, or video games. Ask yourself how that activity might help you handle the problem. For instance, if you enjoy games, maybe you can treat a hard assignment like a level to beat step by step.

Using analogies also makes learning fun. It helps you explain ideas to others in ways they can understand. You might say, "This math problem is like stacking blocks. Each number fits on top of the last one." Suddenly, it feels simple.

Strong problem-solvers use analogies because they connect ideas from everywhere. They don't limit learning to one subject or one way of thinking. They take lessons from nature, art, music, and daily life.

When you learn to use analogies, your brain becomes more flexible. You start to see that solutions often hide in familiar places. You stop saying, "I don't know how," and start saying, "What is this like that I already understand?" That question turns confusion into insight.

Chapter 14: Combine Ideas for Breakthroughs

Sometimes one idea is not enough to solve a problem. The best solutions often come from mixing two or more ideas together. When you combine ideas, you create something new that is stronger than each part on its own.

Think about music. A song sounds richer when you add different instruments. A single note is fine, but when you blend notes, rhythms, and voices, you get a song that feels full. The same rule works for problem-solving. One idea gives you a start. Two ideas together can lead to a breakthrough.

A breakthrough happens when something finally clicks. It often comes after you connect two ideas that did not seem to fit before. Your brain likes to make these connections. It looks for patterns and builds links between things you already know and things you are still learning.

Here's how to combine ideas in a smart way:

1. **Write down all your ideas.**

   Even small or strange ones matter.

2. **Look for pairs that seem unrelated.**

   Ask, "What happens if I put these together?"

3. **Test the mix.**

   See if it solves more of the problem than either idea alone.

4. **Keep adjusting.**

   Sometimes the first mix doesn't work, but another version might.

Here's an example. Suppose your class is trying to make studying more fun. One idea is to use flashcards. Another idea is to play team games. When you combine them, you get a quiz competition where teams use flashcards to earn points. Now learning feels like play.

Combining ideas also helps you when you feel stuck. If one idea does not work, look for another that might fill the gap. You can take parts of two different plans and merge them into one. This works in school, sports, and even friendships. If one way to solve a disagreement fails, mix a second approach that focuses on listening. The blend might solve what neither way could fix alone.

You can practice this skill by picking two random things and finding a way to link them. For example, how could a bicycle and a backpack work together? Maybe you design a bike with a built-in storage bag. The idea may sound simple, but thinking that way trains your brain to see connections.

Here's a short exercise. Pick two problems you faced this week. Write one idea for each. Now ask yourself, "What if I combined them?" For example, if you wanted to save time on homework and also help a friend, you might form a study group. That single idea solves both problems.

Combining ideas is about flexibility. It teaches you that solutions do not need to come from one place. When you mix ideas, you discover that creativity grows through connection, not perfection.

Strong problem-solvers build new things from what already exists. They borrow, blend, and improve. They are not afraid to mix ideas that seem odd together because they know that great answers often live where two different thoughts meet.

When you learn to combine ideas, you stop waiting for perfect inspiration. You start creating it. Every mix you try brings you one step closer to a breakthrough.

Chapter 15: Play with "What If?" Scenarios

Every problem has more than one answer. The trick is to find them. Playing with "What if?" questions helps you imagine different paths before you choose one. It turns problem-solving into an adventure of ideas instead of a race to one solution.

When you ask "What if?", you give yourself permission to explore. You test new thoughts in your mind without risk. It's like trying on clothes before deciding what fits best. You don't have to be right. You only need to be open.

"What if?" questions make your brain flexible. They help you see what could happen if you changed one part of a plan. You can imagine what would go wrong, what would go right, and what might surprise you.

Here's how to use "What if?" scenarios:

1. **Start with the problem.**

   Say it clearly in one sentence.

2. **Change one thing.**

   Ask, "What if I did this instead?"

3. **Picture what would happen next.**

   Think through the steps.

4. **Write down what you learn.**

   Some answers will be silly, but others might reveal a new path.

Here's an example. Your team wants to design a new school poster, but everyone argues about the design. You could ask, "What if we let each person design one version and then vote?" or "What if we combine the best part of each idea?" Suddenly, you have more options and less arguing.

"What if?" thinking is useful when you feel stuck. It pulls your brain out of the same loop and into fresh territory. You might discover that the limits you saw weren't real at all.

You can also use "What if?" questions to test future choices. "What if I studied ten minutes every night instead of one hour before the test?" or "What if we met earlier to plan the project?" Each question gives you new insight into what could work better.

Here's a short exercise. Pick something small that frustrates you, like forgetting homework or rushing in the morning. Write five "What if?" questions about it. For example, "What if I packed my bag the night before?" or "What if I set two alarms instead of one?" One of those answers will likely solve the problem.

When you ask "What if?", you train your brain to think ahead. You learn to see cause and effect before things happen. You also learn that every problem has more than one door, and curiosity helps you find the best one.

Strong problem-solvers don't fear new ideas. They test them safely in their minds first. They imagine outcomes, adjust plans, and find smart paths forward.

Asking "What if?" turns problem-solving from a task into a creative game. It teaches you that you are not stuck with one answer. You always have options waiting to be explored.

Chapter 16: Reverse Engineer the Solution

Sometimes the best way to solve a problem is to start from the end and work backward. This approach is called reverse engineering. It means figuring out how something works by taking it apart or tracing each step in reverse. When you do this, you understand the path that leads to success.

Reverse engineering is common in science, sports, and design. A scientist studies how a machine works by taking it apart piece by piece. A chess player reviews a finished game backward to see which moves led to victory. You can use the same method with any problem.

When you reverse engineer, you ask one question: "If this is where I want to end up, what had to happen right before this?" Then you keep asking that question until you reach the beginning.

Here's how to do it:

1. **Start with your goal.**

   Write it clearly. For example, "Finish my science project by next Friday."

2. **Ask what needs to happen right before that.**

   Maybe it's "test my experiment."

3. **Keep going backward.**

   "To test my experiment, I need to build it." "To build it, I need materials." "To get materials, I need a list."

4. **Write each step in order.**

   Now you have a full plan that shows how to reach your goal.

Let's look at an example. You want to make the school soccer team next season. Start from the end: being chosen for the team. What has to happen before that? You need to perform well at tryouts. What has to happen before that? You need to practice your weak spots. What happens before that? You need to plan your weekly training schedule. Now you know where to begin.

Reverse engineering gives you clarity. It turns a big goal into a line of small, clear actions. It also helps you find what might block your progress. You might see a missing step or something that takes longer than expected. Knowing that early helps you prepare.

Here's a short exercise. Pick a goal that feels far away. Write it at the top of a page. Then work backward step by step until you reach where you are today. Read your list from bottom to top. You now have a roadmap that leads straight to your goal.

Reverse engineering is not guessing. It's learning by looking closely. It teaches you that success has a structure. Every result comes from a series of actions. When you trace those actions backward, you learn exactly what to do next.

Strong problem-solvers don't always start at the beginning. They start at the end, understand what success looks like, and build the path that leads there. When you learn to reverse engineer, you stop feeling lost. You see the whole picture from finish to start, and that makes every goal within reach.

Chapter 17: Challenge Conventional Wisdom

Conventional wisdom is what most people believe to be true. It is the common answer, the usual way, or the rule everyone follows without asking why. Sometimes it works, but not always. Good problem-solvers know how to question what everyone else accepts.

Challenging conventional wisdom means being brave enough to think for yourself. It means asking, "Is this really the best way?" instead of copying what others do. It is not about arguing for the sake of it. It is about checking if the old way still fits the problem you are facing now.

Here is an example. Your school has always held bake sales to raise money. It works, but people are tired of them. You ask, "Why do we always do bake sales?" The answer might be, "Because we always have." That is not a real reason. You suggest a talent show instead. It attracts more people, earns more money, and feels new. You found a better way because you dared to ask one question.

Here is how to challenge conventional wisdom in a smart way:

1. **Identify what everyone believes.**

   Write down the rule or habit that seems automatic.

2. **Ask why it exists.**

   Find the reason behind it. Sometimes it made sense once but not anymore.

3. **Look for evidence.**

   Is there proof that this way still works?

4. **Test your own idea.**

   Try a small version first and see what happens.

You can practice this in everyday life. If your study group always meets after school, ask, "Would mornings work better?" If your sports team always warms up the same way, ask, "Could we try something new?" You are not being rude. You are helping the group think.

Here is a short exercise. Think about one routine you see every day at school or home. Write down what it is and why people do it. Then ask, "Does this still help us, or do we do it out of habit?" Write one new way to try it.

Challenging old ideas does not mean disrespecting them. It means checking if they still serve their purpose. Many great inventions came from people who questioned what others said was impossible.

Strong problem-solvers do not accept "because that's how it's always been" as a final answer. They ask, observe, and test. They know that improvement begins when someone is curious enough to question what everyone else takes for granted.

When you learn to challenge conventional wisdom, you become a better thinker. You see beyond habits and traditions. You look for what truly works instead of what used to work. That is how progress starts, one thoughtful question at a time.

Chapter 18: Steal Like an Artist (Ethically)

But isn't this copying?

No, we're learning from the best and making it our own!

Every creative thinker borrows ideas. The smartest ones borrow wisely. "Stealing like an artist" means learning from others, using their ideas as inspiration, and then making something new that is your own. It is not copying. It is growing from what already exists.

All great thinkers, inventors, and artists learn this early. They study what came before them, understand why it worked, and then change it to fit their own style or purpose. That is how new ideas are born. You do not have to start from nothing. You can build from what others have done.

Think about music. A new song often uses chords or rhythms that already exist. The artist changes the melody, adds new words, or gives it a different beat. The result feels fresh, even though it started with something old. That is what it means to steal like an artist.

Here is how to do it the right way:

1. **Look for good examples.**

   Study people who do what you want to do well. Notice what makes their work strong.

2. **Take ideas, not products.**

   Use their methods, not their exact words or results.

3. **Add your own twist.**

   Change the idea to fit your voice, your problem, or your goal.

4. **Give credit.**

   If someone helped or inspired you, say so. Being honest builds respect.

Here's an example. You are writing a speech for school. You read a famous speech online and notice how the speaker starts with a story, then gives a clear message. You do not copy their story, but you use the same structure. You begin with your own story and build your message around it. You borrowed the pattern, not the words.

You can also apply this in science or design. Suppose you see a robot that picks up boxes. You think, "What if I use the same idea to pick up trash?" You take the same principle but apply it to a new problem. That is ethical creativity, learning by building on others' work.

Here's a short exercise. Think of something you like, a book, a game, or an invention. Write down three things that make it work well. Then write one way you could use those ideas to improve something you are working on.

When you learn from others, your brain grows faster. You see patterns, learn techniques, and develop your own style. Copying teaches you what already exists. Creating from what you've learned teaches you what's possible next.

The key word is *ethically.* Stealing like an artist never means taking credit for someone else's work. It means learning from the best, adding your own ideas, and creating something honest and new.

Strong problem-solvers know that creativity is not about starting from zero. It is about noticing what works and improving it. Every new idea is part of a chain that started long before you. When you add your piece to that chain, you make something that belongs to you.

When you learn to steal like an artist, you stop waiting for perfect inspiration. You start seeing ideas everywhere , in books, music, people, and daily life. You realize that creativity grows when you pay attention, learn with respect, and add your own voice to the mix.

Chapter 19: Diverge, Then Converge

Every creative thinker learns to move in two directions. First, you *diverge*. That means you open your mind, explore many ideas, and welcome every possibility. Then, you *converge*. That means you bring those ideas together, choose what works best, and shape them into a clear plan.

Diverging and converging are like breathing. You breathe out to release, then breathe in to focus. Both steps matter. If you only diverge, you drown in too many ideas. If you only converge, you miss creative ones. Good problem-solvers know when to do each.

Here's how it works. Suppose your class needs to choose a theme for a school play. In the first stage, diverging, you gather as many ideas as possible. "Superheroes," "space travel," "mystery," "school life," "time travel." No idea is too strange. The goal is variety. In the second stage, converging, you group similar ideas and discuss which one fits your goal, time, and resources. You narrow the list until one strong theme remains.

You can use this pattern for any problem. When you face a big question, start wide. Collect information, ideas, and opinions. Then move to focus. Sort what you found, combine related ideas, and remove what doesn't fit.

Here's a simple way to practice:

1. **Diverge first.**

   Spend five minutes writing down every idea that comes to mind. Don't judge or stop. Quantity matters.

2. **Pause and read your list.**

   Notice patterns and connections.

3. **Converge.**

   Pick the top three ideas that seem most useful or realistic.

4. **Test or discuss them.**

   Choose one to move forward with.

Here's another example. You want to improve your study habits. During the diverging stage, you brainstorm: study in groups, make flashcards, set alarms, draw diagrams, use music, take breaks. Later, you converge: you keep flashcards, shorter study sessions, and breaks because they fit your schedule. The rest can wait. You used creativity to explore, then logic to decide.

This skill also helps in group work. In a team, the diverging stage lets everyone speak freely. No one feels shut down. Once the ideas are out, the converging stage helps the group choose what to act on. Everyone feels heard, and decisions happen faster.

Here's a short exercise. Pick a small problem, like organizing your desk. Write ten ideas in two minutes. That's diverging. Then circle two ideas that make the most sense and try them today. That's converging. You'll see how both steps help you think better.

Learning to diverge and converge keeps your thinking balanced. One part of your brain explores. The other part decides. Together, they make your problem-solving stronger.

Strong problem-solvers know that creativity is not wild guessing or quick choosing. It's both. You first open your mind wide, then narrow it with purpose. When you learn to diverge and converge, you stop choosing between imagination and focus. You learn to use both at the right time.

Chapter 20: Gamify the Process

This project taking forever.

Let's turn it into a challenge—whoevever finishes their task first wins a prize!

Work feels lighter when it feels like play. Gamifying the process means turning problem-solving into a game. It helps you stay focused, have fun, and push through hard tasks without getting bored or giving up.

Games have goals, rules, challenges, and rewards. Problem-solving can have the same. When you treat your work like a game, you start to enjoy the challenge instead of fearing it. You turn pressure into motivation.

Here's how to gamify your process:

1. **Set a clear goal.**

   Every game has an objective. Write down what you want to achieve, like finishing your essay or cleaning your room.

2. **Create levels or steps.**

   Break your goal into small parts. Each part is a level you can "win."

3. **Add a timer.**

   See how much you can do in fifteen minutes. Try to beat your score next time.

4. **Give yourself rewards.**

   When you finish a level, treat yourself. It could be five minutes of free time or your favorite snack.

5. **Track your progress.**

   Mark your wins on a chart or in a notebook. Seeing progress keeps you moving.

Here's an example. You need to study for a science test, but you keep losing focus. You decide to turn it into a game. For every ten correct answers, you earn one point. If you reach ten points, you get to watch a short video. Suddenly, studying feels less like a chore and more like a challenge. You end up studying longer without noticing.

Gamifying the process works in groups too. If your class has to clean the playground, turn it into a team game. Split into groups, set a timer, and see who can collect the most trash safely. Everyone wins when the space is clean, but the game makes it more exciting.

Here's a short exercise. Pick one task you've been avoiding. Turn it into a game. Set a goal, break it into steps, and plan a small reward for finishing each step. Try it once and notice how it changes your attitude.

When you gamify your work, you teach your brain to enjoy effort. You start connecting hard work with fun and progress. That mindset will help you in school, sports, and life.

The goal is not to avoid hard things. It's to make them easier to face. A game gives structure, feedback, and small wins that keep you going.

Strong problem-solvers know that attitude matters as much as skill. They find ways to stay engaged, even when the task is tough. Gamifying the process keeps motivation high and energy steady.

When you learn to treat challenges like games, you stop fearing effort. You start chasing improvement. Every point, level, and small win becomes proof that you are growing stronger and smarter.

SECTION 3:
Analytical Thinking

Creative thinking helps you find ideas. Analytical thinking helps you test and shape them. It's the part of problem-solving that uses logic, facts, and careful observation. While creativity asks, "What could work?", analysis asks, "Does this work, and why?"

Analytical thinking doesn't mean you have to be a math expert. It means learning to look closely, spot patterns, and use evidence instead of guesses. When you think this way, you make stronger decisions. You don't depend on luck or opinion, you depend on proof.

In this section, you'll learn how to use data, trace causes, find patterns, and test your ideas. You'll learn to break complex problems into parts that make sense. Each chapter will help you build habits that make your thinking clear, calm, and smart

Chapter 21: Follow the Data Trail

Every problem leaves clues. Those clues are found in facts, numbers, and observations, what we call data. When you follow the data trail, you look carefully at what's real instead of guessing. It's how scientists, engineers, and great thinkers uncover the truth.

Data helps you see what's really going on, not what you *think* is happening. Without it, you risk solving the wrong problem. Following the data trail keeps you honest and focused. It teaches you to think with evidence, not emotion.

Imagine your class keeps running out of art supplies. Some students say it's because people waste them. Others say the teacher doesn't order enough. Instead of blaming, you start tracking what's used each week. You notice that most supplies disappear after group projects. The data shows that big projects, not waste, cause the shortage. Once you see that, you can plan better.

Here's how to follow the data trail step by step:

1. **Start with a clear question.**

    Ask something you can measure, like "Why are we running out of materials so quickly?" or "When are we most productive?"

2. **Collect facts, not opinions.**

    Facts come from counting, observing, or timing events. Opinions come from feelings or guesses. Write facts down exactly as they happen.

3. **Keep your notes organized.**

    Use lists, tables, or charts to record what you find. A simple notebook works fine.

4. **Look for patterns.**

    Ask yourself what repeats. Do certain days, times, or people appear in your notes often? Patterns point to causes.

5. **Draw conclusions carefully.**

    Don't rush. Wait until the facts line up clearly before deciding what they mean.

Here's another example. You think your homework takes too long every night. Instead of complaining, you decide to track it for a week. You write how long each subject takes. By Friday, you see that most of your time goes to reading, not writing. You also notice that you lose focus after 8 p.m. Now you have proof. You can read earlier or break up your study time. The data helps you act wisely.

When you use data, you remove confusion. You stop saying "I feel like this always happens" and start saying "This happens three times a week." That small shift changes everything. Facts give you power to solve the real issue.

Here's a quick exercise. Pick one problem in your daily routine. Maybe you are always late, forget your homework, or lose things. For one week, record what happens and when. At the end of the week, read your notes. What do they show? The pattern you find will often reveal a simple fix.

Following the data trail also builds fairness. When you base decisions on evidence, everyone trusts the outcome more. You are not blaming or guessing; you are showing proof. In teamwork, this builds respect and better communication.

Strong problem-solvers know that data doesn't replace thinking, but it strengthens it. Feelings tell you what matters. Facts tell you what's true. When you combine both, your decisions become clear and steady.

Following the data trail is not about being perfect with numbers. It's about paying attention. It's about noticing what happens, writing it down, and learning from it. When you learn to follow the data trail, you turn small details into big understanding. You stop guessing, start seeing, and make every choice count.

Chapter 22: Use Root Cause Analysis

When a problem keeps coming back, it means you have not fixed the real cause yet. You might have treated the surface, but not the root. Root cause analysis helps you dig deeper to find what is truly behind a problem. Once you fix the root, the problem stays solved.

Think of a weed in a garden. If you cut off the top, it looks gone, but it grows back because the root is still in the ground. To stop it for good, you have to pull out the whole root. Problems work the same way.

Here's a simple way to find the root cause. It's called the "Five Whys." You start with what happened, then keep asking "Why?" until you reach the reason that started it all. It often takes about five questions to get there.

Let's try an example. You forgot to hand in your homework.

1. Why? Because you didn't finish it.
2. Why didn't you finish it? Because you ran out of time.
3. Why did you run out of time? Because you started too late.

4. Why did you start too late? Because you didn't write it in your planner.

5. Why didn't you write it down? Because you were rushing to pack up after class.

Now you see the root cause, you were rushing and didn't track your homework. The fix isn't doing more work. It's slowing down at the end of class and writing your assignments clearly.

Here's another example. Your soccer team keeps losing games. The first reason might be "We don't score enough." But when you ask why, you find the real problem: players don't practice passing, so they lose control of the ball. The fix is not shouting "score more." It's spending time improving teamwork.

Here's how to use root cause analysis:

1. **Start with the main problem.**

   Write it down in one sentence.

2. **Ask "Why?" again and again.**

   Keep digging until you reach a cause that makes sense and can be fixed.

3. **Look for patterns.**

   If the same reason appears in different problems, that's a strong clue.

4. **Plan your fix.**

   Choose one small action that attacks the root, not the surface.

Here's a short exercise. Think about something that frustrates you often. Maybe your backpack is messy, or you always lose pencils. Write the problem down and ask "Why?" five times. When you reach the last answer, write one thing you can do to stop it from happening again.

Root cause analysis helps you think deeper instead of faster. It teaches patience and attention. Instead of reacting to every problem, you slow down and study it.

This kind of thinking makes you better at solving any challenge. You stop wasting time fixing symptoms that will return. You start fixing the real issue.

Strong problem-solvers know that the first answer is rarely the best one. They ask "Why?" until the truth shows up. Once you find the root cause, you have power. You can stop problems before they start again.

When you learn to use root cause analysis, you become a detective of solutions. You learn to look beneath the surface and find what truly needs to change. That's how you turn short fixes into lasting results.

Chapter 23: Find Patterns and Trends

Every problem leaves a trail. When you look closely, you can often see that certain things happen again and again. Those repeated things are called *patterns*. When patterns continue to grow or change over time, they form *trends*. Spotting them helps you understand how problems build and how to stop them before they get bigger.

Patterns are like clues that show you what is normal and what is not. Once you notice a pattern, you can predict what might happen next. You stop being surprised and start being prepared.

Let's look at an example. You notice that you forget your lunch about once a week. You write down the days it happens and realize it's always on Mondays. That's the pattern. The trend shows that Mondays are rushed because you wake up late. Now you can plan to pack your lunch the night before.

Finding patterns helps you make smarter choices. You stop guessing and start seeing. You can use this skill in school, sports, and daily life.

Here's how to find patterns and trends:

1. **Collect information.**

   Write down what happens, when it happens, and how often.

2. **Look for repeats.**

   What keeps showing up? Is there a time, place, or habit that appears again and again?

3. **Ask what the pattern means.**

   Is it good or bad? Helpful or harmful?

4. **Watch how it changes over time.**

   That's your trend. Does it get better, worse, or stay the same?

Here's another example. You're studying for a big test and want to see what helps you remember best. You track your study habits for a week. You find that the nights you review with a friend, you score higher on practice questions. That's a pattern. Over a few weeks, you notice your scores rise every time you use that method. That's a trend. You've found what works, and now you can do more of it.

Patterns are not always easy to spot at first. Sometimes they hide under small details. You might need to collect data for a few days or weeks before the pattern becomes clear. But once you see it, it feels like turning on a light.

Here's a short exercise. Pick one small problem, like being tired in the morning or losing pencils. Track it for five days. Write when it happens and what you were doing right before. Look for what repeats. That pattern is your clue to fixing it.

Patterns can also show good habits. If you notice that you feel more focused when you eat breakfast, that's a trend you want to keep. Not all patterns are problems. Some show what helps you succeed.

Strong problem-solvers watch for signs instead of waiting for surprises. They notice when small things repeat and act early. That saves time and prevents bigger issues later.

When you learn to find patterns and trends, you start thinking like a scientist. You collect clues, look for order, and use logic to make smart choices. Patterns tell you what has been happening. Trends tell you where things are heading. Together, they help you shape what happens next.

Chapter 24: Use Decision Trees for Clarity

Every choice leads somewhere. Some paths work well, and others don't. When a problem has many options, it can feel confusing to pick the right one. A decision tree helps you see your choices clearly before you act. It's a simple tool that turns messy decisions into a picture you can understand.

A decision tree looks like a map. You start with one question or problem at the top. Each branch shows a choice you could make. From each choice, new branches grow to show what could happen next. When you draw it out, you see how one decision leads to another. It helps you think ahead and stay calm instead of guessing.

Let's take an example. Imagine you're choosing what to do this weekend. Your problem is, "How can I use my time wisely?" You draw a small box at the top with that question. From it, you draw three branches: "Study," "Hang out with friends," and "Rest." Under "Study," you add two branches: "Finish homework" and "Review for a test." Under "Rest," you add "Sleep in" and "Go outside." When you look at the full picture, you can compare which choice helps you most right now.

Decision trees are useful for both small and big problems. They help you slow down and see every option. They also show the results that follow each one, so you can make decisions that fit your goal.

Here's how to make your own decision tree:

1. **Write your main question.**

   Keep it clear, like "Which club should I join?"

2. **List your options.**

   These become your first branches.

3. **Add what happens next.**

   Write what might result from each choice. Be honest about both good and bad outcomes.

4. **Look at the full picture.**

   Which path leads closest to your goal? Which one has too many risks?

5. **Choose with confidence.**

   Once you see the map, the best option often stands out.

Here's another example. Your teacher gives you the choice to do a group project or work alone. You draw your decision tree. Under "Work alone," you list that you can control the schedule but have more work. Under "Group project," you note that you share tasks but need to coordinate with others. Seeing both sides helps you choose what fits you best.

Here's a short exercise. Think of a decision you need to make this week. Maybe what to do after school or how to spend your weekend. Write your question in a box. Then draw two or three branches with your options. Under each one, write what could happen if you chose that path. Look at your tree and decide which outcome feels best.

Decision trees make you think clearly instead of reacting quickly. They show that every choice has results. You can't control everything, but you can see where your choices might lead. That helps you plan ahead instead of feeling lost later.

Strong problem-solvers use tools to organize their thinking. They don't let choices pile up in their minds. They put them on paper, look at them, and decide. A decision tree doesn't make the decision for you. It shows you the road so you can choose where to go.

When you learn to use decision trees, decisions stop feeling scary. You start to see each option as a path, and you choose with calm and confidence. Clarity turns pressure into direction, and direction leads to progress.

Chapter 25: Apply Pareto's Principle (80/20 Rule)

Sometimes a few small things make the biggest difference. Pareto's Principle, also called the 80/20 Rule, teaches that about 80 percent of results come from 20 percent of the effort. It means that not everything you do has the same impact. Some actions matter much more than others.

Learning this rule helps you spend time wisely. You focus on what truly counts instead of trying to do everything at once. When you find the few actions that create the biggest results, you solve problems faster and with less stress.

Let's look at an example. You have ten subjects to study, but your grades are lowest in two. By focusing extra time on those two, you might raise your overall average more than if you studied everything equally. That's the 80/20 Rule in action. A small part of your effort (20 percent) leads to most of your progress (80 percent).

Here's how to use Pareto's Principle in daily life:

1. **Find what matters most.**

    Ask yourself, "Which parts of this problem have the biggest effect?"

2. **Measure your results.**

   Notice which actions lead to real progress and which only fill time.

3. **Focus your energy.**

   Put more time into the few things that give strong results.

4. **Don't chase perfection.**

   Some small details don't need your full effort. Save your energy for what makes the biggest change.

Here's another example. Imagine your soccer team wants to win more games. You track your plays and see that most goals come from quick passes near the goal line. That's your 20 percent. So you spend more practice time improving those passes instead of working on less important drills. Soon, the team's score improves.

You can use this principle with chores, schoolwork, or hobbies. If you have a messy room, you might notice that most of the mess comes from a few things, maybe clothes and papers. Cleaning those areas first gives you an 80 percent improvement with 20 percent of the effort.

Here's a short exercise. Think of something that feels overwhelming, like studying for a test or planning an event. Write down all the tasks involved. Then circle the two or three that make the biggest difference. Start with those. Once they're done, see how much easier the rest feels.

The 80/20 Rule helps you see that effort isn't equal. Working harder is good, but working smarter is better. You don't have to fix everything.

You have to fix the parts that matter most.

Strong problem-solvers know how to find the small actions that lead to big results. They look for patterns, test ideas, and focus their time where it counts. This skill saves energy and builds confidence.

When you learn to apply Pareto's Principle, you stop wasting time on tasks that don't move you forward. You start putting effort where it matters. A small change in focus can make a big difference in results. That's how smart thinkers get more done with less struggle.

Chapter 26: Test Your Hypothesis

A *hypothesis* is a smart guess. It's what you think might be true before you have proof. Scientists use hypotheses every day to test their ideas, but you can use them too in school, sports, or daily life. Testing your hypothesis means checking if your guess actually works. It's how you turn ideas into knowledge.

When you face a problem, your first thought is often a theory about why it's happening. Maybe you think, "I get low grades because I study too late at night." That's your hypothesis. You test it by changing one thing, like studying earlier for a week, and then see what happens. If your grades improve, your guess was right. If not, you try something else.

Testing a hypothesis helps you think like a scientist. You don't assume your first idea is correct. You use evidence to find out. This way, your choices become stronger and less random.

Here's how to test a hypothesis:

1. **Start with a clear question.**

   What are you trying to figure out? Example: "Why do I get tired during class?"

2. **Make your best guess.**

   Think of one reason. Maybe, "Because I stay up too late."

3. **Plan a test.**

   Change one thing connected to your guess. Go to bed earlier for a week.

4. **Observe what happens.**

   Keep track of results. Do you feel more awake?

5. **Decide what you learned.**

   Was your guess right or wrong? Either answer teaches you something.

Here's an example. You think your basketball shots miss because you stand too far from the hoop. You form your hypothesis: "If I shoot from closer, I'll score more." You test it during practice. You shoot from different spots and count how many go in. The data shows that your shots are better from mid-range. Now you know what to practice most.

Here's another example for school. You believe that background music helps you study better. You test it. For three nights, you study with music. For three nights, you study in silence. You notice you remember more facts when it's quiet. You learned something useful, even if your guess was wrong.

Here's a short exercise. Pick a small problem, like losing focus while doing homework. Write your question: "Why do I get distracted?" Then write your hypothesis: "Because my phone is nearby." Test it. Do your homework without your phone for three days and compare how much you finish.

Testing a hypothesis teaches patience and honesty. It's okay if your guess is wrong. A wrong guess is not failure, it's information. Each test gets you closer to the truth.

Strong problem-solvers don't rely on luck. They make careful guesses and test them. They learn from every result. That's what makes them reliable thinkers.

When you learn to test your hypothesis, you stop saying "I think so" and start saying "I know because I tested it." You learn that real understanding comes from proof, not guessing. And once you can test your ideas, you can improve almost anything, one smart guess at a time.

Chapter 27: Use Comparative Analysis

When you face a choice between two or more options, it helps to compare them carefully. Comparative analysis means looking at each option side by side to see which one works best. It helps you make decisions based on facts, not feelings.

Comparing things is something you already do every day. You compare foods when choosing lunch, movies when deciding what to watch, and routes when getting to school. Each choice depends on what matters most to you. Comparative analysis turns that habit into a clear method you can use for solving problems.

Here's how to use comparative analysis:

1. **List your options.**

   Write down what you are deciding between.

2. **Choose your criteria.**

   Decide what makes one choice better than another. Criteria could be time, cost, effort, or quality.

3. **Score each option.**

   For each criterion, give a simple score or note.

4. Look at the results.

See which option meets more of your goals or gives the best balance.

Here's an example. You are choosing between two after-school activities, soccer and art club. Your criteria are fun, time, and learning. Soccer is high on fun, but takes a lot of time. Art club is flexible and helps you learn new skills. When you compare both, you see that art club fits your schedule better right now. You made a smart decision based on facts, not impulse.

Comparative analysis works well for group decisions too. Suppose your class is choosing which charity to support. You list three options and your criteria: community impact, cost, and student involvement. Each group researches and shares what they find. When you compare, one charity stands out as the best match for your goals. The decision feels fair because everyone can see how it was made.

Here's another example. You want to buy a new backpack. Instead of picking the one that looks coolest, you compare them. One has more space, another is cheaper, and another is stronger. You rate them by price, comfort, and quality. The strongest one scores highest overall, so you choose it. You avoided a quick decision by looking at all the facts.

Here's a short exercise. Think of a decision you need to make soon, like what book to read or what game to play. Write two or three options. Then list three things that matter most to you. Score each option from one to five for each thing. The choice with the highest score is probably your best one.

Comparative analysis helps you see clearly. You learn to weigh options instead of reacting to them. It keeps you from being swayed by emotion, pressure, or habit.

Strong problem-solvers use this method to stay objective. They know that when choices are written down and compared, the right one often appears on its own.

When you learn to use comparative analysis, you stop guessing what might work. You start seeing what does work. You base your decisions on logic, not luck, and that makes every choice smarter and more confident.

Chapter 28: Correlation vs. Causation

CORRELATION ≠ CAUSATION

Ice Cream Sales

Shark Attacks

Sometimes two things happen at the same time, and it looks like one caused the other. But that is not always true. *Correlation* means two things are connected. *Causation* means one thing makes the other happen. Knowing the difference helps you think clearly and avoid wrong conclusions.

Many people mix these up. They see two things happen together and assume they are related. But just because two things happen at the same time does not mean one caused the other.

Here's an example. You notice that on days you wear your lucky shoes, you score more points in basketball. That is correlation, the two things happen together. But the shoes do not cause the points. The real cause might be that you practiced more or slept better.

You can also see this in school. Imagine the class gets better grades when the weather is nice. Does the sunshine cause better grades? No. The nice weather might make everyone feel happier and more focused, which leads to better work. The connection is indirect.

Here's how to tell the difference between correlation and causation:

1. **Collect data carefully.**

   Write down what happens and when.

2. **Look for patterns.**

   Notice which things appear together.

3. **Ask if one event truly affects the other.**

   Could there be another reason both happen?

4. **Test your idea.**

   Change one thing and see if the other changes too. If it does, you may have found causation.

Here's an example you can try. You think listening to music while studying helps you remember facts. To test it, you study with music for three days and without music for three days. If your scores only improve with music, that shows causation. If they stay the same, it was only correlation.

Here's another. You notice that when your class gets extra recess, everyone behaves better. That could be causation, more playtime might release energy, helping students focus later. But it could also be correlation if extra recess happens only on calm days when everyone is already relaxed. You would need to test it to know.

Here's a short exercise. Think of two things that often happen together in your life. Write them down. Then ask yourself, "Does one cause the other, or do they just happen at the same time?" Try to find another explanation.

Learning this difference helps you make smarter choices. You stop believing in coincidences and start searching for real reasons. You become careful about what you assume and what you can prove.

Strong problem-solvers always ask questions before deciding what is true. They do not rush to connect events.

They check, test, and verify. That is how they find what is real and what only looks real.

When you understand correlation and causation, you protect yourself from mistakes. You see that not every connection means cause. You learn to look deeper before deciding what the truth is. That skill keeps your thinking sharp and your decisions fair.

Chapter 29: Solve for Variables

A variable is something that can change. In math, it is often shown as a letter like *x* or *y*. In problem-solving, a variable is any part of a situation that affects the result. When you learn to find and control your variables, you gain power to shape outcomes instead of being surprised by them.

Every problem has variables. Some you can control, and some you cannot. Knowing the difference helps you focus your energy. The goal is to understand how each variable changes the result. Once you do, you can test ideas, make predictions, and find solutions that work more often.

Here's an example. You are trying to bake cookies, but they keep turning out too hard. What are your variables? The baking time, oven temperature, ingredient amounts, or mixing method. You change one thing at a time, maybe lower the temperature, and see what happens. If the cookies turn out soft, you found the key variable.

You can use the same thinking in school or sports. Imagine your test scores go up and down each week. You ask yourself what changes each time. Do you sleep less on some nights? Do you study with friends on others? Each of those is a variable. When you find which one affects your results, you can use it to improve.

Here's how to solve for variables in any problem:

1. **List what could change.**

   Write down all the parts that might affect the result.

2. **Choose one variable to test.**

   Keep everything else the same.

3. **Observe the outcome.**

   If the result changes, that variable is important.

4. **Record what you learn.**

   You may find more than one variable that matters.

Here's another example. You are trying to wake up on time. The result is whether you get to school early or late. The variables could be bedtime, alarm volume, or when you set your backpack out. If you test one variable, going to bed earlier, and you start arriving on time, you know what made the difference.

Here's a short exercise. Pick a simple problem from your week, like not finishing homework or feeling tired after lunch. List three variables that might affect it. Then test one change and write what happens. Over time, you'll see which variable matters most.

Solving for variables teaches you to think like a scientist. You don't fix everything at once. You adjust one thing, observe, and learn. This kind of thinking helps you make smarter choices because it's based on cause and effect, not luck.

Strong problem-solvers look for variables instead of blaming themselves or others. They say, "What can I change?" instead of "Why does this always happen?" That small shift gives them control.

When you learn to solve for variables, you turn confusion into clarity. You understand why results change and how to make them better. Every experiment, decision, and habit becomes easier to improve because you know which parts to adjust and which to leave alone. That's how smart thinkers build steady progress, one tested variable at a time.

Chapter 30: Simplify the Math

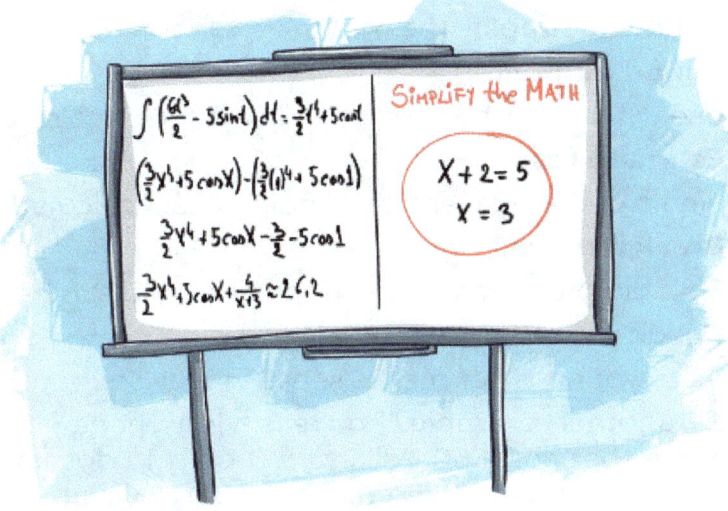

Numbers are everywhere. You use them when you count, plan, measure, and compare. But sometimes, numbers can feel too big or too complicated. When that happens, the best thing to do is simplify the math. Simple math helps you see the problem clearly and make quick, smart choices without getting lost in details.

Simplifying math does not mean avoiding it. It means breaking it into smaller, easier parts. You focus on what matters most and leave out what does not change the answer. This way, you save time and stay confident instead of feeling stuck.

Here's an example. You are planning a bake sale for your class. You want to know how much money you could earn. The complicated way would be to count every flavor, every price, and every cost in detail. The simple way is to start with an estimate. You plan to sell 50 cookies for 2 dollars each. That means 100 dollars total. Then you subtract about 20 dollars for ingredients. Your quick math shows that you'll make around 80 dollars. You didn't need a calculator, you needed clear steps.

Simplifying the math helps you focus on the goal. You learn to look for patterns instead of perfection. You can use this skill in school, sports, or even planning your day.

Here's how to simplify the math:

1. **Round numbers.**

   Use whole numbers instead of small decimals.

2. **Estimate first.**

   Find a quick answer before doing exact calculations.

3. **Break it down.**

   Split big problems into smaller steps you can handle.

4. **Check your logic.**

   Ask if your answer makes sense in real life.

Here's another example. You're saving money to buy a video game that costs 60 dollars. You earn 10 dollars a week for chores. Instead of calculating every week, you can estimate: six weeks of saving should be enough. If you save a little extra, you'll reach your goal sooner. Simple math keeps your plan easy and doable.

Simplifying math also helps with time management. If your project is due in 10 days and you have 5 parts to complete, that's about 2 parts every 4 days. Breaking it down like that makes it feel manageable. You no longer see one big task; you see small steps you can finish on time.

Here's a short exercise. Think of a problem that involves numbers, maybe planning your allowance, counting homework hours, or estimating travel time. Write the numbers down, round them, and find a simple way to calculate. Then check if your quick answer is close to the exact one. You'll see how often a simple estimate gets you close enough to plan well.

Simplifying math builds confidence. You stop fearing numbers because you know how to handle them. You learn that good problem-solvers don't always do hard math, they do smart math.

Strong problem-solvers look for the simplest path to the right answer. They don't overthink. They use numbers to guide choices, not to overwhelm themselves.

When you learn to simplify the math, you make decisions faster, plan better, and think more clearly. You stop worrying about being perfect and start using math as a tool for progress. Numbers become your friends, not your obstacles.

SECTION 4:
Strategic Approaches

Strategy means thinking ahead. It is how you plan your moves before acting. When you use strategy, you don't rush into problems. You step back, look at the full picture, and decide where to focus your time and energy.

Being strategic is not about doing more. It is about doing what matters most and doing it in the right order. It helps you stay calm in complex situations and make choices that work now and later.

In this section, you will learn how to plan backward, think ahead, and prepare for surprises. You will also learn to balance quick wins with long-term goals. Strategy turns smart thinking into smart action.

Chapter 31: Plan Backward from Success

When most people plan, they start from the beginning. They ask, "What should I do first?" Strategic thinkers flip the question. They start from the end and work backward. They ask, "What does success look like, and what must happen before that?" This method is called backward planning.

Planning backward helps you see the steps that truly matter. You focus on what leads to the goal, not what keeps you busy. It's like walking a maze from the exit to the entrance. You find the fastest route because you already know where you want to end up.

Here's an example. You want to finish your science project by Friday. You start by writing your final goal: "Project ready to present on Friday." Then you ask what needs to happen right before that. "Finish poster by Thursday." Before that? "Print results by Wednesday." Before that? "Run experiment by Tuesday." Before that? "Gather materials by Monday." You've built your plan backward, one step at a time.

Backward planning works for all kinds of goals, from schoolwork to personal habits. It gives you a timeline that makes sense because each step supports the next.

Here's how to plan backward from success:

1. **Write your goal clearly.**

    Make it one sentence that shows what "done" looks like.

2. **List what must happen right before that.**

    Keep working backward until you reach today.

3. **Add time for surprises.**

    Leave room for mistakes or changes.

4. **Follow the plan in reverse.**

    Start from the first step and move forward again, checking off each one.

Here's another example. You want to perform in a school play next month. Start with the goal, being ready for opening night. Then think backward. You need to memorize lines before rehearsal week. Before that, you need to read the full script. Before that, you need to get your role. Now you know your first step: audition with confidence.

Here's a short exercise. Pick one goal you want to reach in the next two weeks. Write it at the top of your page. Then ask, "What must happen before this?" Keep asking until you reach today. That's your roadmap.

Planning backward keeps your eyes on the result. You waste less time on distractions and stay focused on what truly moves you forward.

Strong problem-solvers know that success is not luck. It's built step by step with clear thinking and careful timing. When you plan backward, you make sure every action leads directly to your goal. You start where others finish, and that makes you one step ahead.

Chapter 32: Think Like a Chess Player

Chess is all about planning ahead. Every move shifts what comes next. Great players don't hurry, they consider what might happen several turns in advance. Problem solvers can learn much from this. Thinking like a chess player means planning your next steps carefully and guessing how others will react.

By thinking ahead, you stay ready. You stop scrambling at the last moment and start shaping what will occur. You rely on patience, logic, and awareness, not chance.

Here's how to think like a chess player:

- Look ahead. Before acting, ask yourself what could happen next.
- Consider others. How might people respond to your choice?
- Plan a few moves. If your first plan doesn't work, what's next?
- Stay flexible. If things change, adapt without losing sight of your goal.

For example, say you have a group project due soon. Instead of waiting until the last minute, you plan ahead. You list tasks, assign roles, and schedule meetings. You also think about what might go wrong, like someone missing their part, and decide to check progress early. This simple step stops bigger issues later.

Another example: during a soccer match, you see a teammate running to the goal. Instead of kicking the ball right away, you look up, predict where they'll be, and pass there. You planned ahead, and it worked.

Thinking like a chess player means keeping your options open. You're not stuck on one plan. You see the big picture and stay calm even when things change.

Try this: think of something coming up this week, a test, game, or busy day. Write down your plan. Then ask what could go wrong and what you'd do if it does. Now you have a backup plan, like a chess player thinking ahead.

This mindset helps you face challenges confidently. You fear surprises less because you thought them through. You stop guessing and start planning.

Strong problem solvers use this skill everywhere. They imagine different outcomes, make smart choices, and stay ready for change.

When you think like a chess player, you see life as a series of smart moves. Each choice builds on the last. You learn patience, focus, and balance. You might not win every time, but you always play smartly.

Chapter 33: Leverage Opportunity Costs

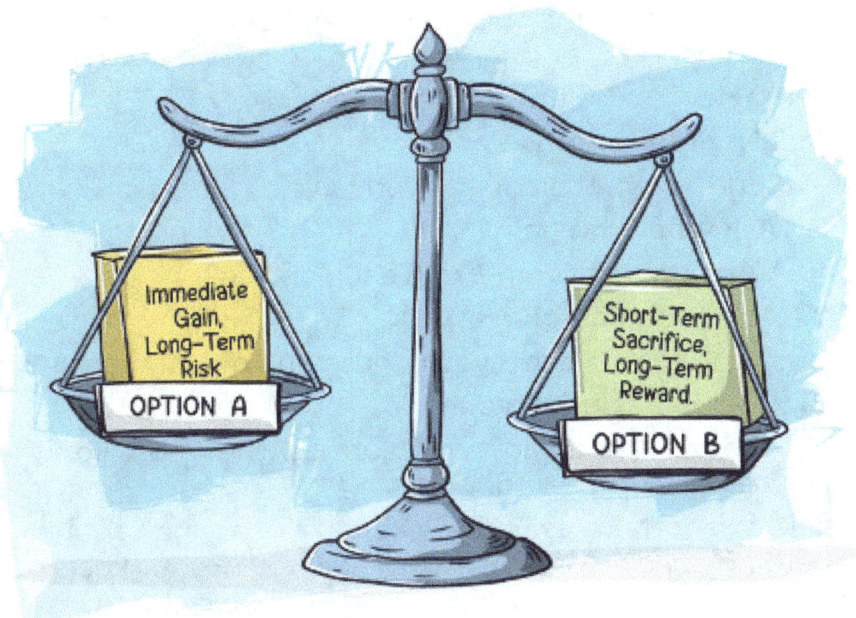

Every choice has a cost. When you pick one thing, you give up something else. That trade is called an *opportunity cost*. Understanding it helps you make smarter decisions because you learn to see what each option is worth, not only what you gain but also what you lose.

Opportunity cost is not about money alone. It's about time, energy, and focus. You can spend only so much of each, so choosing wisely matters. Every "yes" to one thing is also a "no" to something else.

Here's an example. You have two options after school: join the soccer team or take a coding class. If you choose soccer, you get exercise and teamwork. If you choose coding, you learn new skills but lose practice time. The opportunity cost of each choice is what you give up by not choosing the other. When you think about that, your decision becomes clearer.

You can apply this thinking to almost any situation. Imagine you have one free hour. You could spend it watching videos or working on a project. Watching videos might be fun, but you lose the progress you could have made. Working on your project gets you closer to your goal, but you give up a break. Both choices are fine, but good thinkers understand what each one costs.

Here's how to use opportunity costs wisely:

1. **List your options.**

   Write down the choices you have.

2. **Ask what you gain.**

   What benefits come with each choice?

3. **Ask what you give up.**

   What do you lose if you choose one over the other?

4. **Decide based on value.**

   Choose the option that brings the most long-term benefit or meaning.

Here's another example. You are saving money for something special. You can buy a new toy now or keep saving for a bike later. The opportunity cost of buying the toy is losing your chance to get the bike. Once you see that clearly, you can decide what matters more.

Opportunity costs are not always easy to see. Sometimes the thing you give up is invisible, like rest, energy, or focus. That's why it helps to pause and think before deciding. Ask, "If I say yes to this, what am I saying no to?" That question changes how you make choices.

Here's a short exercise. Think of something you chose recently. Maybe you spent your weekend on one activity instead of another. Write down what you gained and what you missed. Would you make the same choice again? Why or why not?

Learning to see opportunity costs helps you use time and energy wisely. You start thinking about the value of each choice, not just the excitement of the moment.

Strong problem-solvers understand that every decision has trade-offs. They do not try to do everything. They focus on what matters most and accept what they must give up. That makes their decisions calm and confident.

When you learn to weigh opportunity costs, you stop guessing and start choosing with purpose. You think before saying yes, and that single habit can make every part of your life more balanced and rewarding.

Chapter 34: Identify Key Leverage Points

A leverage point is a small action that creates a big result. It's the place in a system where one smart change can shift everything for the better. Good problem-solvers look for these points first because they make the biggest difference with the least effort.

Think of leverage like using a seesaw. If you push down on one end, the other end rises. The secret is knowing where to push. The same rule applies to problems. When you find the right spot to act, you move the whole situation with less force.

Here's an example. Your class keeps arguing during group work. You could try to fix every argument one by one, but that takes time. Instead, you notice that most problems start when no one knows who is leading. You suggest choosing a leader at the start of each project. That one small change improves every group task afterward. You found a leverage point.

Here's how to find leverage points:

1. **Understand the system.**

   Look at how different parts connect. Who does what? What depends on what?

2. **Find what repeats.**

   Problems often come from the same place each time. That place is usually where the leverage lies.

3. **Ask what small change could help the most.**

   Focus on one action that makes other problems easier to solve.

4. **Test your idea.**

   Try it on a small scale first. If it works, you can expand it.

Here's another example. You keep running late for school. You try many fixes, faster breakfast, quicker showers, but nothing sticks. Then you realize the real issue happens the night before. You go to bed too late. By changing that one thing, you wake up rested and move faster. The small change fixes a big problem.

You can also find leverage points in learning. If you struggle with studying, track where you lose focus. Maybe it's when your phone is nearby. Turning it off during homework becomes your leverage point. It's simple, but it unlocks better results.

Here's a short exercise. Think of a problem that feels too big. Write down all the parts that cause it. Then ask yourself, "If I changed just one thing, which would make the biggest difference?" That's your leverage point.

Finding leverage points makes you efficient. You stop wasting time on things that don't matter. You act where it counts. Over time, you start noticing that small, smart moves can lead to large, lasting improvements.

Strong problem-solvers know that they don't need to fix everything. They find the one part of the problem that affects the rest. They focus there until the whole system improves.

When you learn to identify leverage points, you gain quiet power. You stop pushing hard everywhere and start pushing smart where it matters most. That's how big changes begin, with one clear, well-placed step.

Chapter 35: Map the System (Systems Thinking)

Every problem exists inside a system. A system is a group of parts that work together. When one part changes, the others often change too. Systems thinking helps you see how everything connects so you can solve problems that last instead of fixing the same issue again and again.

Most people look at problems in pieces. Systems thinkers look at the whole picture. They ask how one part affects another. This way, they understand how small actions can cause big results later.

Here's an example. Imagine your school cafeteria always runs out of food early. You might think the problem is that students take too much. But if you look closer, you might notice that the food delivery is late, or that lunch schedules overlap. When you map the system, you see that the cause is not only the students but also timing, planning, and supply. Seeing the full system helps you fix the real issue.

Here's how to think in systems:

1. **Identify all the parts.**

   Write down everything connected to the problem. Include people, tools, places, and rules.

2. **Draw the links.**

   Show how one part affects another. Use arrows or lines to connect them.

3. **Find feedback loops.**

   Notice where actions repeat or build on each other.

4. **Spot weak points.**

   Look for where the system breaks down most often. That's where you can make the biggest impact.

Let's look at another example. Your group project keeps falling behind. You map the system: group members, meeting times, communication tools, deadlines, and feedback from your teacher. Then you notice that meetings often start late because no one checks the schedule. The missing link is a reminder system. Adding a group chat reminder fixes the chain and keeps the system working smoothly.

Here's a short exercise. Think of a small system in your life, maybe your morning routine. Write down every step from waking up to leaving the house. Then mark where problems often appear. Maybe it's finding your shoes or packing your bag. Once you see the full picture, you can adjust the part that slows you down.

Systems thinking helps you understand cause and effect over time. It reminds you that no problem stands alone. When you fix one part of a system, you can make many things better at once.

Strong problem-solvers use systems thinking to prevent future problems. They look at how choices today will affect tomorrow. They ask questions like, "If we change this rule, what else will change?"

When you learn to map the system, you stop guessing. You see how everything fits together and where to act. This kind of thinking turns quick fixes into lasting solutions. You start seeing problems not as single events but as patterns that can be shaped for good.

Chapter 36: Scenario Planning for Uncertainty

No one knows the future. Things change fast, and sometimes problems appear that you didn't expect. Scenario planning helps you prepare for what could happen, not only for what you hope will happen. It is a way to think ahead and stay ready, even when the future is unclear.

A scenario is a story about what might happen. It is not a prediction. It is a way to test your plans against different situations so you are not surprised when something changes. Scenario planning teaches you to stay flexible and calm when things shift.

Here's an example. You are organizing a school fair. You hope for a sunny day, but what if it rains? You make two scenarios. One plan is for sunshine, outdoor games and food stalls. The other plan is for rain, move activities to the gym. When the day comes, you don't panic. You already know what to do.

Here's how to use scenario planning:

1. **Start with your goal.**

   What are you trying to achieve?

2. **List what could change.**

   Think about what might go right, wrong, or differently.

3. **Create a few scenarios.**

   Write short "what if" stories, like "What if we run out of time?" or "What if someone gets sick?"

4. **Plan your responses.**

   For each scenario, write what you would do.

5. **Review and adjust.**

   If something new happens, add it to your list for next time.

Here's another example. You are preparing for a big test. You plan to study every evening, but you also imagine other scenarios. What if you get sick? You plan to review short notes instead of long chapters. What if you lose power at home? You plan to study at the library. These small plans keep you from falling behind.

Here's a short exercise. Pick one event in your week, like a class trip or sports game. Write down three "what if" questions about what could go wrong. Then write one action you could take for each. When the day comes, you'll feel more confident because you already thought about the possibilities.

Scenario planning is not about worrying. It is about being smart with your choices. It helps you think before trouble starts and stay steady when it does.

Strong problem-solvers don't try to control the future. They prepare for it. They think ahead, make flexible plans, and adapt when things change. That is what makes them dependable and calm under pressure.

When you learn to plan for different scenarios, you stop feeling afraid of surprises. You start trusting yourself to handle them. You learn that uncertainty is not the enemy — it is a teacher that helps you grow stronger and wiser.

Chapter 37: Build in Redundancy

Redundancy means having a backup. It is the extra plan, tool, or resource you keep in case something goes wrong. Building in redundancy helps you stay safe, steady, and ready when things do not go as planned.

Most people think they will not need a backup. Smart problem-solvers know that mistakes, delays, and surprises happen. Redundancy keeps small problems from turning into big ones. It gives you a second chance to stay on track.

Here's an example. You are working on a school project that is due next week. You save your file on your computer, but you also email a copy to yourself. If your computer stops working, you still have your work. That second copy is your redundancy.

Here's how to build in redundancy:

1. **Expect that something might fail.**

    Ask, "What could go wrong?"

2. **Prepare a second option.**

    Keep a spare tool, plan, or resource ready.

3. **Test your backups.**

    Make sure they work before you need them.

4. Keep things simple.

Too many backups can be confusing. Choose the most useful ones.

Here's another example. You are preparing for a school play. The main actor is sick. Luckily, you already practiced with an understudy who knows the lines. The show continues because you built in redundancy.

You can use this thinking anywhere. In sports, teams train extra players for every position. In school, you might keep an extra pencil in your bag. At home, your family might have spare batteries for the flashlight. Redundancy is everywhere once you look for it.

Here's a short exercise. Think of something important you do every week. Then ask, "If my plan fails, what will I do instead?" Write down your backup. That one step can save you stress later.

Building redundancy does not mean expecting failure. It means respecting reality. It means being ready for the unexpected so you can keep moving forward.

Strong problem-solvers use redundancy to stay confident under pressure. They are not afraid of change because they have already thought about what to do if things go wrong.

When you learn to build in redundancy, you become more reliable. You stop worrying about every small risk because you have a plan that protects your progress. One small backup can keep everything else standing. That is the quiet strength of thinking ahead.

Chapter 38: Focus on Long-Term Impact

Every choice you make today shapes what happens tomorrow. Focusing on long-term impact means thinking beyond the quick result. It means asking how your actions will affect you, others, and your goals in the future. Smart problem-solvers think this way because they know that short-term wins do not always lead to lasting success.

Many people act fast to fix problems right away. They want to feel better now. Sometimes that helps, but often it only hides the problem. When you focus on long-term impact, you slow down and choose what will keep working later. It takes patience and foresight, but it builds stronger results.

Here's an example. You have a big test coming up. Staying up all night to study might help you remember a few more facts, yet you'll be too tired to think clearly in the morning. Going to bed early and studying steadily all week gives you better results in the long run. The first choice feels good for a moment, the second one lasts longer.

Focusing on long-term impact teaches you to see beyond today. You start to notice patterns. You start to value consistency over speed. Every small decision becomes part of something bigger: your habits, your character, your growth.

Here's how to think long-term:

1. **Ask future questions.**

   What will this decision look like in a week, a month, or a year?

2. **Look for lasting benefits.**

   Does this choice build strength or only bring comfort for now?

3. **Balance short and long goals.**

   You can enjoy small wins while still working toward bigger ones.

4. **Review your results.**

   Look back at what worked before and repeat what gave steady progress.

Here's another example. Your class decides whether to plant trees or decorate the playground for an event. Decorating will look nice for one day. Planting trees will make the school better for years. When you focus on long-term impact, you see that small acts today can grow into something lasting.

Here's a short exercise. Write down one thing you do every day, like checking your phone, studying, or playing sports. Ask yourself how it will help you six months from now. If it does not move you toward your goals, think of one way to change it.

Focusing on long-term impact helps you use your time wisely. You stop chasing what feels urgent and start building what truly matters. You learn to care more about growth than about quick fixes.

Strong problem-solvers know that big goals take time. They make choices that build over days, weeks, and years. They stay patient, steady, and focused on results that last.

When you learn to think this way, you stop solving problems for the moment and start solving them for good. Each thoughtful choice becomes a building block for your future. That is how real progress begins, with actions that stand the test of time.

Chapter 39: Prioritize Quick Wins

Big goals can feel heavy when you start. They take time, focus, and effort. Quick wins help you build momentum. A quick win is a small success that gives you confidence and moves you forward. It reminds you that progress is possible even when the goal is large.

Quick wins are not shortcuts. They are small steps that show your plan is working. Each one makes the next step easier. When you collect small wins, you build trust in yourself and your team. That motivation helps you keep going until you reach the finish line.

Here's an example. You want to clean your entire room, but it looks too messy to start. Instead of trying to do everything at once, you focus on one small area, like your desk. You finish it quickly and feel proud. That small victory gives you energy to clean the rest. The same method works for schoolwork, sports, and personal goals.

Quick wins matter because they show visible progress. You do not have to wait weeks to feel successful. You can celebrate small improvements right away. This builds momentum, which keeps you moving.

Here's how to find quick wins:

1. **Start small.**

   Choose one part of the problem that you can fix today.

2. **Pick something visible.**

   Choose a step where you can clearly see the result.

3. **Act quickly.**

   Complete it in a short amount of time.

4. **Celebrate progress.**

   Recognize the win and use that energy for the next step.

Here's another example. Your group needs to create a presentation for class. The project feels too big. You decide to finish the title slide and outline on the first day. Once that part is done, everyone feels more organized. That quick win creates momentum for the rest of the work.

Here's a short exercise. Think of one goal that feels too large right now. Break it into three small tasks. Choose the one you can finish today. Complete it, then take a moment to notice how it feels to move forward.

Quick wins also help teams work better together. When people see early results, they stay positive and focused. Small successes remind everyone that progress is real and that effort matters.

Focusing only on long-term goals can feel tiring. Quick wins keep energy high while the bigger plan unfolds. They turn big problems into a series of smaller, manageable steps.

Strong problem-solvers know that steady progress beats sudden perfection. They look for early wins that keep the team engaged and motivated. They use each success as a signal that the plan is working.

When you learn to prioritize quick wins, you turn big challenges into a series of easy starts. You stay motivated, your confidence grows, and your goals stop feeling out of reach. Every big victory begins with one small, well-earned win.

Chapter 40: Think Incrementally

Thinking incrementally means making progress one small step at a time. Instead of trying to reach your goal all at once, you move forward in steady, measured steps. Each small improvement builds on the last until you achieve something big. This kind of thinking helps you stay patient, calm, and focused.

Many people quit because they expect instant results. When progress feels slow, they give up. Incremental thinkers know that real change takes time. They understand that even the smallest step counts as progress when it moves you closer to your goal.

Here's an example. You want to learn to play guitar. If you expect to play full songs right away, you will feel frustrated. If you learn one chord a week, you will be playing songs in a few months. Each small piece matters. That is the power of incremental progress.

Thinking incrementally teaches you to see improvement everywhere. It helps you stay positive because you notice growth instead of waiting for perfection. You start to see that success is built through practice, not speed.

Here's how to think incrementally:

1. **Set small goals.**

    Break your big goal into smaller parts you can finish soon.

2. **Measure your progress.**

    Keep track of what you complete each day or week.

3. **Adjust as you go.**

    If one step feels too hard, make it smaller and keep moving.

4. **Celebrate milestones.**

    Notice every improvement, even the tiny ones.

Here's another example. You want to read more books this year. Instead of aiming to read fifty books, you set a goal to read ten pages every day. After a few weeks, you realize you have already finished one book. Small daily steps lead to big results.

Here's a short exercise. Pick one goal that feels too large, like organizing your room or saving money. Break it into small steps. For cleaning, start with one shelf each day. For saving, put away a little money each week. Watch how these small actions add up over time.

Thinking incrementally also helps you stay flexible. If something changes, you can adjust your next step without losing sight of your goal. You stay in control because you always know what to do next.

Strong problem-solvers know that big leaps are rare, but small steps are steady. They trust the process. They keep moving even when progress feels slow, because they know that consistency creates success.

When you learn to think incrementally, you stop chasing quick results. You start building lasting progress. Every small action becomes part of something bigger. Over time, those steps add up to something strong, finished, and real. That is how great problem-solvers reach their goals, one clear step at a time.

SECTION 5:
Collaborative Problem-Solving

Some problems are too big to solve alone. That is why teamwork matters. Collaborative problem-solving means using the strengths of many people to reach the best answer together. It teaches you how to listen, share ideas, and work toward one clear goal.

Working with others does not mean giving up your own thoughts. It means learning how to combine your ideas with theirs. When people think together, they see what one person alone might miss. Collaboration turns individual effort into shared success.

In this section, you will learn how to build trust, balance viewpoints, and make fair group decisions. You will also learn how to lead, communicate, and handle conflict with respect. Solving problems as a team takes patience, but it makes your solutions stronger and more complete.

Chapter 41: Harness the Power of Teamwork

A team is more than a group of people. It is a group with a shared goal. Teamwork works best when everyone brings their skills, effort, and ideas to support that goal. When people work together with respect and purpose, they can solve problems faster and better than any one person can alone.

Teamwork begins with understanding. Each person has something valuable to offer. Some people plan well, others organize, and others bring creative ideas. When these strengths come together, the group becomes stronger.

Here's an example. Your class needs to design a poster for an event. One student is good at drawing, another is good at writing, and another is great at organizing materials. Working together, you create a poster that looks good, reads clearly, and is finished on time. Alone, each piece might be weaker. Together, they work perfectly.

Here's how to harness the power of teamwork:

1. **Share a clear goal.**

   Make sure everyone understands what the team is trying to achieve.

2. **Know your roles.**

   Let each person focus on what they do best.

3. **Communicate often.**

   Talk about progress, ask questions, and give updates.

4. **Support one another.**

   Help teammates when they struggle and celebrate when they succeed.

Here's another example. You are on a soccer team preparing for a big game. The defenders, midfielders, and forwards each play different roles. When everyone stays in position and trusts each other, the team works smoothly. When one person tries to do everything, the system breaks down.

Here's a short exercise. Think of one time you worked on a group project. Write down what worked well and what did not. Then write one thing you could do differently next time to make the team stronger.

Teamwork does not mean everyone always agrees. It means everyone stays focused on the shared goal, even when opinions differ. Strong teams respect each other and stay open to learning from mistakes.

Strong problem-solvers know how to work with others. They understand that teamwork multiplies strength. They give credit freely and take responsibility when needed.

When you learn to harness the power of teamwork, you realize that success grows when people trust and help each other. You learn that one person's strength can fill another's weakness, and that together, you can achieve far more than you could alone.

Chapter 42: Listen Before Solving

Good problem-solvers know that real understanding comes before action. Listening is the first and most important step in solving any problem. When you listen, you learn what others think, feel, and need. Without that, you might fix the wrong thing or make a choice that does not work for everyone.

Listening means paying attention, not waiting for your turn to speak. It means trying to understand the whole picture before deciding what to do. Many people skip this step because they want to move fast. They hear part of the story and rush to fix it. That leads to confusion, hurt feelings, and wasted effort.

Here's an example. A group in your class is upset because their science project isn't working. One person says the materials are wrong, another says the instructions are unclear, and another says no one followed the plan. Instead of jumping in with a solution, you ask questions. You listen to each person and repeat back what you hear. Soon, you discover that everyone was using different versions of the instructions. The problem wasn't the materials, it was communication. By listening first, you found the real cause.

Listening is not the same as agreeing. You can understand someone's point of view without accepting it. The goal is to hear what is true for them so you can make a fair and informed choice.

Here's how to listen before solving:

1. **Stay quiet.**

   Let the other person finish before you speak.

2. **Look and focus.**

   Give your full attention. Avoid distractions.

3. **Ask questions.**

   Say things like "Can you tell me more?" or "What do you mean by that?"

4. **Repeat what you hear.**

   Say it back to check that you understood correctly.

5. **Pause before reacting.**

   Take a moment to think before giving advice or making decisions.

Here's another example. A friend is frustrated about a group project. You want to help right away, but instead you listen carefully. You learn they don't want advice, they just need someone to understand. Listening helps them calm down and think clearly again. Sometimes, listening is the best solution by itself.

Here's a short exercise. This week, try to listen closely during one conversation. Don't interrupt or offer ideas right away. Wait until the person is finished, then summarize what they said in your own words. You'll be surprised how much you learn.

Listening before solving makes every part of teamwork stronger. It builds trust because people feel heard. It also helps you make smarter choices because your decisions are based on facts, not assumptions.

Strong problem-solvers use listening as a tool, not a delay. They know that understanding others saves time in the long run. Listening helps uncover hidden issues, prevent mistakes, and bring people together.

When you learn to listen before solving, you start solving problems at the right level. You see the real need, not the noise around it. You become the kind of person others trust who is calm, thoughtful, and fair. And that is where true problem-solving begins.

Chapter 43: Balance Diverse Perspectives

Every person sees the world in a different way. Each view comes from their own experiences, background, and ideas. When you bring people together to solve a problem, those differences become a strength. Balancing diverse perspectives helps a team find creative and fair solutions that work for more people.

It can be tempting to listen only to the voices that sound like your own. That feels comfortable, but it limits growth. When you invite different opinions, you see parts of the problem you might have missed. You also learn how your own ideas fit into a bigger picture.

Here's an example. Your class is planning a school event. Some students want a talent show, while others want a sports day. At first, it feels like no one agrees. Then you listen to everyone's reasons. The talent show group wants something fun indoors. The sports group wants something active outdoors. When you combine both ideas, you plan a full day that starts with sports in the morning and ends with a talent show in the afternoon. The event works better because you balanced many viewpoints.

Balancing perspectives does not mean making everyone happy. It means giving everyone a fair chance to be heard, then finding what connects their ideas. When you do that, the solution becomes stronger and more complete.

Here's how to balance diverse perspectives:

1. **Invite input.**

    Ask for opinions from everyone, not only the loudest voices.

2. **Listen with respect.**

    Even if you disagree, try to understand why someone thinks that way.

3. **Look for overlap.**

    Find what different ideas have in common.

4. **Combine strengths.**

    Mix the best parts of each idea into one stronger plan.

5. **Stay focused on the goal.**

    Keep reminding the group of what you are trying to achieve together.

Here's another example. In a group project, one person prefers detailed planning while another likes to start quickly. Both have value. Planning helps avoid mistakes, and quick action helps the group make progress. When you balance both, you plan enough to stay organized and move fast enough to meet deadlines.

Here's a short exercise. Think about a time when you disagreed with someone. Write what they said and what you said. Then write one thing from their view that could make your own idea better.

Balancing perspectives teaches patience. It reminds you that your idea is not the only one that matters. Sometimes, the best solution sits between two viewpoints. When people feel heard, they work harder and trust each other more.

Strong problem-solvers know that diversity of thought brings better results. They don't choose sides too quickly. They look for connections that make everyone's ideas stronger.

When you learn to balance diverse perspectives, you stop seeing differences as barriers. You start seeing them as tools for better thinking. You realize that no one has every answer alone, but together, every answer is within reach.

Chapter 44: Build Consensus with Stakeholders

Working in a team means making decisions that everyone can support. *Consensus* happens when a group agrees on one plan after listening to each other. It does not mean everyone gets exactly what they want. It means everyone helps shape the decision and feels okay with the final choice.

A *stakeholder* is anyone who is affected by the decision. In school, that could be classmates, teachers, or parents. In a club, it could be team members and leaders. When you build consensus, you make sure all voices are heard before moving forward. This builds trust and teamwork.

Here's an example. Your class needs to choose a theme for a fundraiser. Some people want a movie night, others want a bake sale. Instead of voting right away, you talk it through. You list the pros and cons of each idea, ask for suggestions, and combine them. The group agrees to host a movie night that also sells snacks. Everyone feels part of the decision because they were included.

Building consensus takes time, but it helps avoid arguments later. When people help decide, they care more about making the plan work.

Here's how to build consensus step by step:

1. **Include everyone.**

    Make sure all voices are heard, even the quiet ones.

2. **Share the goal.**

    Remind everyone what you are trying to achieve together.

3. **Discuss options.**

    List every idea without judging.

4. **Find common ground.**

    Look for parts that most people agree on.

5. **Agree on one plan.**

    Choose the option that fits the goal and feels fair to the group.

Here's another example. Your team is deciding how to divide tasks for a big project. Everyone has different preferences. One person likes research, another enjoys design, and another prefers presenting. You talk as a group until each person feels comfortable with their role. The project runs smoothly because everyone agreed on the plan together.

Here's a short exercise. Think of a time when your group had to choose between two ideas. How did the group make the choice? Did everyone feel heard? If not, what could have helped build agreement?

Building consensus helps you become a fair teammate and a thoughtful leader. It teaches you to listen, respect others, and find shared solutions instead of pushing your own way.

Strong problem-solvers know that decisions made together last longer. They bring people into the process instead of leaving them out. They make sure everyone feels ownership of the outcome.

When you learn to build consensus, you turn a group into a team. You stop arguing about who is right and start focusing on what is best. That kind of teamwork creates not only good results but also stronger friendships and mutual respect.

Chapter 45: Use Structured Decision-Making

Every group faces moments when a choice must be made. Some decisions are easy, but others feel messy because there are too many opinions or too much information. Structured decision-making helps teams stay organized. It turns guessing into a clear process that leads to fair, thoughtful results.

Making decisions in a group can be tricky. People have different ideas, emotions, and priorities. Without structure, decisions can drag on or cause tension. A clear process helps everyone know how choices will be made and what steps to follow.

Here's an example. Your class needs to choose a new recycling plan. Some students want separate bins, others want color-coded bags. Instead of arguing, your teacher suggests a structured process. You list all the options, discuss the pros and cons, and then vote. The group follows the plan and reaches a decision that feels fair to everyone.

Here's how to use structured decision-making:

1. **Define the problem.**

   Write down what decision needs to be made. Keep it short and clear.

2. **Gather information.**

   Collect facts, opinions, and possible solutions.

3. **List all options.**

   Make sure every idea gets a chance to be heard.

4. **Set criteria.**

   Decide what makes an option good: cost, time, effort, or quality.

5. **Compare the options.**

   See which ones meet the criteria best.

6. **Make the choice.**

   Vote, agree by discussion, or let the group leader decide based on input.

7. **Review the result.**

   After trying it, check if the choice worked well.

Here's another example. Your school club wants to spend its saved money. The group has three ideas: buy new uniforms, plan a trip, or donate to charity. You set your criteria: what helps the club most, what fits the budget, and what supports your values. When you compare options, you find that donating to charity wins by the criteria. The group feels proud of the final choice because it was made fairly.

Here's a short exercise. Think about a time when your group struggled to make a decision. Write how the choice was made. Then write how using steps like listing options or setting criteria could have helped.

Structured decision-making does not take away creativity. It keeps it balanced. It gives everyone a voice while keeping the process focused. It helps teams move forward instead of getting stuck in endless discussion.

Strong problem-solvers use structure when the group feels confused or divided. They know that a clear method builds trust and speeds up progress. They also check results afterward to see what can be improved next time.

When you learn to use structured decision-making, you turn group choices into shared victories. You replace confusion with clarity and opinion with evidence. You help teams make fair, smart decisions that everyone supports. That kind of structure builds stronger teamwork and lasting success.

Chapter 46: Avoid Groupthink

When people work in groups, they often want to get along. They want to agree quickly and keep the peace. That sounds good, but sometimes it leads to a problem called *groupthink*. Groupthink happens when a team agrees too fast and stops thinking carefully. People hold back their real opinions because they don't want to cause disagreement.

Groupthink feels easy in the moment, but it creates weak decisions. The group may miss better ideas, overlook risks, or choose something that doesn't work well. Avoiding groupthink means creating space for honest discussion, even when opinions differ.

Here's an example. Your class is choosing a design for a school T-shirt. The first person suggests a blue shirt, and everyone agrees right away. No one wants to seem difficult. Later, you realize that half the students prefer red. The group rushed to agree and ignored other views. A better discussion would have led to a design that everyone liked more.

Avoiding groupthink means making sure every voice is heard. It also means reminding the team that disagreement is healthy when it helps the group think deeply.

Here's how to avoid groupthink:

1. **Invite different opinions.**

   Ask everyone what they think, especially quiet members.

2. **Question early ideas.**

   Do not accept the first answer without exploring others.

3. **Ask for reasons.**

   When someone gives an opinion, ask why they believe it.

4. **Create a safe space.**

   Make it clear that disagreement is not rude — it is useful.

5. **Review before deciding.**

   Pause to check if everyone truly agrees or is just going along.

Here's another example. Your debate team is preparing for a competition. Everyone wants to use the same argument they used last time. One teammate speaks up and says the topic is different, so the plan might not work. The group discusses it, tests new ideas, and ends up with a stronger argument. By allowing disagreement, they avoid groupthink and improve their chances of winning.

Here's a short exercise. Think about a group decision you joined recently. Did you speak your full opinion, or did you stay quiet to fit in? Write what might have changed if everyone had shared their true thoughts.

Avoiding groupthink takes courage and respect. It means caring more about making the right choice than making a quick one. When people feel safe to speak honestly, the group becomes smarter and stronger.

Strong problem-solvers welcome challenge. They listen to all sides, even when it slows things down. They know that true teamwork comes from honesty, not silence.

When you learn to avoid groupthink, you become a leader who values truth over comfort. You help your team think deeply, question wisely, and make decisions that last. Real unity comes from shared understanding, not from quiet agreement.

Chapter 47: Delegate and Share Responsibility

Working in a team means sharing both the effort and the success. No one can do everything alone. Delegating responsibility means dividing tasks so that everyone contributes and the work gets done faster and better. When a team learns to share responsibility, each person feels trusted and valued.

Delegation does not mean giving away work you don't want to do. It means matching the right task to the right person. Everyone has strengths, and good teams use those strengths wisely. One person may be great at planning, another at speaking, and another at organizing. When you delegate well, you let each person shine where they do best.

Here's an example. Your group is creating a short film for a school project. Instead of one person trying to write, record, and edit everything, you divide the work. One student writes the script, another handles the camera, and another edits. Each person owns their part, and the final project looks polished because everyone focused on what they do well.

Here's how to delegate and share responsibility:

1. **Know the goal.**

   Make sure everyone understands what the team is trying to achieve.

2. **Identify strengths.**

   Match people to tasks that fit their skills and interests.

3. **Assign clearly.**

   Explain what each person is responsible for and when it is due.

4. **Trust your teammates.**

   Let them handle their part without constant checking.

5. **Stay connected.**

   Have regular updates to see how everyone is doing.

Here's another example. You are leading a fundraiser. You divide the roles into planning, decorating, and collecting donations. Each person handles their part, but you all meet once a week to check progress. By sharing responsibility, no one feels overloaded and the event runs smoothly.

Here's a short exercise. Think of a group activity you joined recently. Write what tasks each person did. Were the jobs shared fairly? If not, how could the group have divided them better?

Delegation also builds leadership. When you trust others with real responsibility, they grow more confident. It shows that you believe in their abilities. At the same time, you learn how to guide, support, and coordinate without taking over.

Strong problem-solvers know that teamwork means balance. They give clear directions but also listen and adapt. They understand that success belongs to everyone, not only the leader.

When you learn to delegate and share responsibility, your team becomes more efficient and motivated. Everyone feels ownership of the goal, and that makes the work lighter and the results stronger. Shared effort turns ordinary groups into real teams, where every member matters and every job contributes to success.

Chapter 48: Seek External Expertise

Sometimes a team cannot solve a problem on its own. When that happens, it helps to ask someone with more experience or knowledge. Seeking external expertise means finding people outside your group who can offer advice, teach new skills, or give a fresh point of view. Asking for help is not a weakness. It shows that you care about finding the best answer.

Even the smartest teams reach limits. A scientist asks another expert for advice. A sports team listens to a coach. A student asks a teacher for guidance. These moments build understanding and help the group grow stronger.

Here's an example. Your class is designing a school garden, but no one knows which plants grow best in your area. Instead of guessing, you invite the school gardener to share advice. You learn which plants need shade and which need sunlight. With that information, your plan improves. You still do the work, but you use knowledge from someone who knows more.

Here's how to seek external expertise:

1. **Know what you need.**

   Be clear about the question or skill your team is missing.

2. **Find the right person.**

   Look for someone with experience in that topic.

3. **Ask respectfully.**

   Explain your project and what kind of help you are looking for.

4. **Listen carefully.**

   Pay attention to the advice and take notes.

5. **Apply what you learn.**

   Use the new information to make your plan better.

Here's another example. You are part of a robotics team, but your robot keeps losing power. You ask the science teacher for help. They explain how to balance battery weight and power use. Your team fixes the issue and performs better in the next round. Asking for help saved time and taught everyone something new.

Here's a short exercise. Think of a project you worked on that was difficult. Write down one thing an expert could have helped you with. Then write who you might ask next time if you face a similar problem.

Seeking help builds confidence, not dependence. You learn that everyone needs guidance sometimes. It also teaches humility, patience, and curiosity. You start to see that knowledge is everywhere, and learning from others makes you better at solving problems yourself.

Strong problem-solvers know they don't have all the answers. They look outside their group when they need new information. They use what they learn to make better decisions and then share it with others.

When you learn to seek external expertise, you become a better learner and a stronger teammate. You stop feeling stuck because you know where to turn for help. Asking the right questions brings new ideas, new skills, and better solutions for everyone.

Chapter 49: Communicate Solutions Effectively

Finding a good solution is only half the job. The other half is explaining it clearly so everyone understands and supports it. Communicating solutions effectively means sharing your ideas in a way that is simple, honest, and easy to follow. When you do this well, people listen, ask good questions, and work together to make the plan succeed.

Good communication helps a team stay united. If people do not understand the solution, they may feel left out or confused. Clear communication prevents that. It turns an idea into action because everyone knows what to do and why it matters.

Here's an example. Your class decides to start a recycling program. The plan makes sense, but no one remembers which bins are for which materials. You realize the problem is not the plan — it's communication. You make simple posters with pictures and short words. Soon, everyone follows the system easily. The solution works because you explained it clearly.

Here's how to communicate solutions effectively:

1. **Know your audience.**

   Think about who you are speaking to and what they need to understand.

2. **Use simple language.**

   Avoid long sentences and difficult words.

3. **Be clear about steps.**

   Explain what needs to happen first, next, and last.

4. **Check for understanding.**

   Ask questions to make sure everyone follows.

5. **Use visuals if needed.**

   Pictures, charts, or examples can help make things clear.

Here's another example. Your group finishes a science project and needs to present it to the class. Instead of reading the report word for word, you show a short slide with pictures and key facts. You speak slowly, explain how you found your answer, and end by thanking the class for listening. Everyone understands your work because you focused on being clear, not fancy.

Here's a short exercise. Think of a time you explained something to a friend or family member. Did they understand right away, or did you need to explain again? Write what helped them understand and what you could do differently next time.

Communicating well also means listening to feedback. Sometimes people will have questions or concerns. Be patient and answer respectfully. Their input can help improve your solution even more.

Strong problem-solvers do not keep ideas to themselves. They share them clearly and kindly so others can join in. They speak with purpose and listen with care. They know that communication is not about talking the most — it's about making sure everyone is on the same page.

When you learn to communicate solutions effectively, you make teamwork smoother and results stronger. You help others see what you see and believe in what you are doing.

Clear communication turns smart ideas into real action. That is how good thinking becomes real-world success.

Chapter 50: Resolve Conflicts Constructively

Every team faces conflicts now and then. It's normal. People think differently, have their own opinions, and work in unique ways. Conflict itself isn't a bad thing; it shows people care about what they're working on. What really counts is how the team deals with it. Handling conflict well means working through disagreements calmly and fairly, so everyone can keep moving forward together.

If conflicts are ignored or handled badly, it hurts teamwork. People stop listening, get upset, and lose focus. But when handled with respect, conflict becomes an opportunity to learn and get stronger as a team. It builds trust and helps find better solutions.

For example, imagine two students in your group both want to lead a class project. They start arguing. You step in and remind everyone that the main goal is to finish the project well. The group talks it over and decides to split leadership duties—one handles scheduling, the other manages communication. The argument turns into cooperation because everyone focused on fixing the problem, not blaming each other.

Here's how you can deal with conflicts in a positive way:

- Stay calm. Take a deep breath before you speak. Getting angry makes it hard to listen.
- Hear both sides. Let everyone share their view without interruptions.
- Find common goals. Remind the team what you all want to achieve together.
- Choose fair solutions. Look for answers that help the whole team move forward, not just one person "winning."
- Agree and move on. Once the conflict is settled, let it go and focus on what's next.

Another example: during a group assignment, one person feels like they're doing too much work. Instead of arguing, they have a quick talk. Everyone explains what they're doing, and they realize the tasks aren't split evenly. They rework the plan, making it fair for all. This problem was solved through honest and caring conversation.

Try this: remember a time you disagreed with a friend or classmate. How did you respond? What helped calm things down? Write down one thing you could do differently next time to keep the conversation respectful.

Resolving conflict doesn't mean avoiding tough talks. It means facing them with kindness. You can disagree without being rude and stand your ground without hurting feelings. Finding this balance helps everyone feel heard and respected.

People who are good at solving problems don't fear conflict. They know that different opinions can lead to better ideas. They listen, find common ground, and keep their eyes on the goal instead of just arguing.

When you learn to handle conflicts positively, you help build peace and trust. You make teamwork stronger because everyone knows disagreements will be dealt with fairly. Every time you handle a conflict the right way, you bring your team closer and get it ready to succeed.

Conclusion: Problem-Solving Is a Lifelong Adventure

Problem-solving is something you'll use every day, for your whole life. It helps you think clearly, make better decisions, and face challenges with confidence. Every problem you run into is really just a chance to learn more about yourself and the world.

You've now explored lots of ways to solve problems—asking good questions, being creative, looking at data, making plans, and working with others. Think of these as puzzle pieces. When you put them all together, you can handle almost anything calmly and thoughtfully.

Keep in mind, problem-solving never really ends. Even grown-ups are still figuring it out! The goal isn't to have all the answers but to stay curious, think things through, and keep trying until you find a solution that works.

Here's a simple example: Imagine you're building a tower with blocks. It falls down a few times. Instead of quitting, you watch carefully and notice the base is too small. You fix it, and the tower stands tall. That's problem-solving—that moment when you notice, think, test, and improve.

Some quick tips to remember:

- Stay calm. Problems feel less scary when you pause and breathe first.
- Ask questions. Curiosity lets you see things others might miss.

- Keep learning. Mistakes are just new lessons in disguise.
- Work as a team. Together, problems become easier to solve.
- Take small steps. Big goals always start with one tiny move.

Try this: Think about one problem you solved this week, no matter how small. Maybe you fixed a mistake, helped a friend, or found a faster way to get something done. Write down what you did and what you learned. That's how you get stronger, day by day.

Great problem-solvers don't give up when things get tough. They keep thinking, asking, and trying new things. They know every challenge is a chance to practice patience and creativity.

When you start seeing problems as puzzles instead of roadblocks, life gets a lot more fun. Every challenge you figure out gives you more confidence for the next one. Little wins add up to big progress.

So keep practicing. Keep asking yourself, "What's the next step?" and "How can I do this better?" Problem-solving isn't just a skill—it's a way of thinking that grows with you. And the more you practice, the stronger and wiser you become.

Appendix A: Practice Scenarios – Applying Problem-Solving Techniques

These short scenarios give you a chance to practice what you have learned. Each one is a real-life situation where you can use the problem-solving steps from the book. Read each problem carefully, think through what you would do, and decide which technique fits best. There are no perfect answers, what matters most is how you think.

Scenario 1: The Group Project Mix-Up Your group is making a presentation, but two people forgot to finish their slides. The project is due tomorrow. What steps could your team take to stay calm, fix the issue, and still present on time?

Scenario 2: The Lost Homework You worked hard on your homework, but you cannot find it before class. What questions should you ask to find the real cause of the problem? How can you prevent it from happening again?

Scenario 3: The Overbooked Afternoon You have soccer practice, a birthday party, and homework all in one day. You cannot do everything. How can you use prioritizing and planning to decide what to do first?

Scenario 4: The Disagreement with a Friend Your best friend wants to play a video game, but you want to go outside. How can you use listening, empathy, and compromise to find a solution that works for both of you?

Scenario 5: The Broken Science Experiment Your class experiment did not work. Everyone feels disappointed. What steps could you take to find the root cause of the problem and fix it for next time?

Scenario 6: The School Event Rainstorm Your class planned a picnic, but now it's raining. How can you use scenario planning to keep the event fun, even with bad weather?

Scenario 7: The Missing Supplies Your art club runs out of paint halfway through a project. What creative problem-solving steps could you take to finish your work without stopping completely?

Scenario 8: The New Student Challenge A new student joins your class but feels shy and left out. How can your class use teamwork and empathy to make them feel welcome?

Scenario 9: The Messy Morning Routine You keep arriving late to school because mornings feel rushed. What kind of system or plan could you build to make mornings smoother?

Scenario 10: The Online Mix-Up You accidentally send a message to the wrong group chat. How can you take responsibility, communicate clearly, and solve the problem respectfully?

How to Practice:
1. Choose one scenario each day.
2. Write the main problem in one sentence.
3. Ask questions to understand the cause.
4. Pick one or two techniques from the book to solve it.
5. Review your result and think about what you would do differently next time.

Each time you practice, you get a little better at solving problems calmly, clearly, and creatively.

Appendix B: Problem-Solving Checklist

Use this checklist as a guide whenever you face a problem. It will help you stay focused and choose the best steps for the situation.

Step 1: Understand the Problem What exactly is happening? What do I know for sure? What do I still need to find out? Who is involved or affected?

Step 2: Ask Good Questions What is the real problem, not just the surface issue? Why does it matter? What assumptions am I making?

Step 3: Brainstorm Ideas What are all the possible solutions? Have I asked others for ideas or help? Which ideas seem creative or different?

Step 4: Analyze and Test What are the pros and cons of each option? What could go wrong? What does the data or evidence say? Have I tested my idea or checked my plan?

Step 5: Make a Decision Which solution fits the goal best? Do I understand what steps come next? Have I talked to everyone who needs to agree?

Step 6: Take Action Do I have everything I need to start? Have I shared my plan clearly with others? Am I ready to adjust if something changes?

Step 7: Reflect and Improve Did my solution work as planned? What did I learn from this problem? What will I do differently next time?

Keep this checklist somewhere you can see it, in your notebook, on your desk, or near your study space. Every time you face a challenge, walk through each step. The more you use it, the easier problem-solving becomes.

Solving problems is not about being perfect. It's about staying curious, thinking carefully, and taking small, steady steps toward better choices. With practice, you'll be ready for any challenge that comes your way.

Here's another book by Quinn Voss that you might like

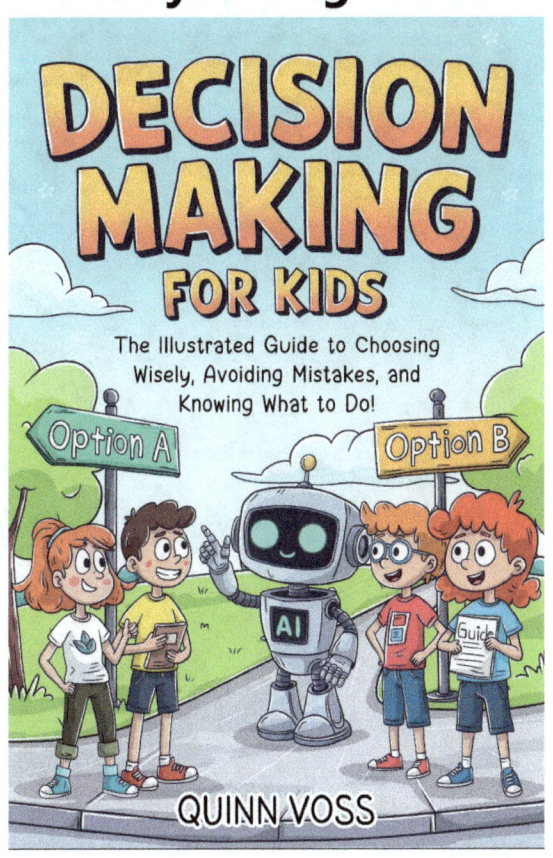

www.ingramcontent.com/pod-product-compliance
Lightning Source LLC
Chambersburg PA
CBHW071513120626
46550CB00006B/2212